ANDREW THOMAS POWELL

Grenville

———— *and the* ————

Lost Colony of Roanoke

THE FIRST ENGLISH COLONY OF AMERICA

Matador
5 Weir Road
Kibworth Beauchamp
Leicester LE8 0LQ, UK
Tel: (+44) 116 279 2299
Fax: (+44) 116 279 2277
Email: books@troubador.co.uk
Web: www.troubador.co.uk/matador

ISBN 978 1848765 962

British Library Cataloguing in Publication Data.
A catalogue record for this book is available from the British Library.

Typeset in 11pt Garamond by Troubador Publishing Ltd, Leicester, UK
Printed and bound in Great Britain by TJI Digital, Padstow, Cornwall

Matador is an imprint of Troubador Publishing Ltd

CONTENTS

List of Illustrations

Acknowledgments

I give thanks to the 'lost' colonists Edward and Winifred Powell, for if it had not been for their being namesakes, I would probably never have read the story of Roanoke. I also give thanks to Sir Richard Grenville, for providing the inspiration and determination never to give up, even under the most trying circumstances.

Acknowledgments go to the Lost Colony Research Group in America (more information on which is available at: http://www.rootsweb.ancestry.com/~molcgdrg/) of whose principals I thank Roberta Estes, for her constant energy in driving our quest ever forward, and for her considerable editorial help on the subject of DNA research. Nelda Percival for keeping my contributions to the project in order; Anne Poole and Mr. George Ray, to whom I am grateful for getting me to the Outer Banks to help look for the colonists, and for both providing such fine "southern hospitality" on this most extraordinary journey. Thanks too, to Scott Dawson for providing such a lively and questioning debate about the subject matter, and to his wife Maggie for welcoming us into the family home.

Here in England, I give thanks to archaeologists Professor

Mark Horton and Louisa Pittman of Bristol University. Their enthusiasm for the project has been of great comfort. Given that in our first foray during November 2009 they endured the tail end of Hurricane Ida, it was surprising that they joined me again in April 2010, only to then experience a week's delay in being able to return to the UK because of an erupting volcano in Iceland. Archaeologists are made of hardy stuff!

Thanks too must go to Jane Seiter, my copyeditor, whose understanding of the English language, encouragement and guidance, has added so much more to this book.

And finally, I have come to understand why so many writers dedicate books to loved ones. For countless hours I have sat here thrashing away on the laptop without so much as a cursory word to my wife, Amanda, sitting on the sofa opposite me, nor indeed to my son, on whose own future I should be concentrating. As my year in office as Mayor of Bideford ends and as this book is finally written, so shall I devote more time to those who have been more than all the things a man should have a right to expect his family to be.

Notes on Transcriptions:

1> In Chapters Two to Eleven inclusive, the transcriptions are 'as written' in the original Hakluyt editions. From this, readers may deduce subtle differences in the style of writing. This strongly suggests that Richard Hakluyt may have simply copied some of the accounts verbatim from original documents.

2> For continuity, the transcribed chapters have been placed here in their correct chronological sequence.

3> All transcriptions use modern English as the basic language but retain the grammar and emphasis of the original. Paragraphs used are arbitrary, purely to make the reading experience less intensive (they were not used in the original transcripts).

4> The Transcripts contain a number of obsolete words and descriptions. To aid the reader, modern day interpretations are included. These, along with some additional commentaries, are written in italics, at the end of each chapter and cross referenced to a number inserted in brackets at the relevant point. E.g [12].

5> All Native American terms, such as personal, natural, or geographical names, have been transcribed exactly as written in the original text.

BM · John White's paintings.
Hakluyt – Elizabethan historian
Mark Horton @ Bristol Uni.
Archivos der Indies
Quinn, David – The Roanoke
                              Voyages

Quick Timeline
1584 – Exploratory voyage
1585 – Military Colony
1586 – Raleigh evacuates,
        Grenville leaves more men
1587 – First colonists arrive .

Introduction

The story of the first attempt to colonise America by the English nation is a story of extraordinary courage, despair, misfortune, joy, and simple wonder. The purpose of this book is to recount all that is known of those voyages and to try to untangle what was an extraordinary period in English history. If you take this book home with you, then prepare for an adventure no Hollywood producer could hope to conjure in their wildest dreams, and remember, as you read, that this is a true story.

The story of how I came to write this book however, has to begin a great many years ago when I found myself peering at some of the 113 known drawings of an obscure artist called John White during a visit to the British Museum. Then, as now, they provided a fascinating and revealing picture of a civilisation that had encountered 'white man' probably for the first time, a civilisation that never knew it was playing the principal role in Britain's first attempt to colonise America. Although this attempt is commonly thought to have been fruitless, it may yet prove to have succeeded—and in doing so, may come to rewrite American history.

The colony that those Native American Indians became

so entwined with was what is now known as the Lost Colony of Roanoke. That colony, in reality, was simply a victim of circumstance and an extraordinary sequence of events that conspired to thwart every attempt to support its foothold in what is now the United States of America.

These attempts at colonisation took place between 1584 and 1590, following a grant given by the royal court of Queen Elizabeth I to Sir Walter Raleigh. The grant permitted Raleigh to set up a colony in what he christened 'Virginia'. This task was to take place fully twenty years before Jamestown, and thirty-three years before the *Mayflower* set sail from Plymouth.

John White's drawings and the colony became an interest for me for years, not least because my family surname appeared among the list of the 'lost'. Yet I was a teenager when I first saw those drawings, and life has a habit of moving on and reprioritising according to the whims of fate. Mine moved on to reprioritise on marriage, a child and civic duty. Thus the memories of reading about the Lost Colony became but mists in the back of my mind. Until two fateful events occurred within months of each other some twenty-five years later.

First, in October 2006, a gentleman from Manteo, the town that is situated on the generally accepted site of the Lost Colony, arrived at my hometown of Bideford. His mission was to present the town with a gift marking twenty years of twinning, an event they had instigated having already researched the Lost Colony connection between us many years previously.

Rather embarrassingly, the town had no record of the twinning. This embarrassment was, of course, food for the media, too, who quickly labelled Bideford 'The town that forgot it was twinned'. Perhaps if it had not done so, though, several of its more dynamic councillors may never have put together a plan to visit Manteo to find out more.

The second fateful event occurred when Professor Mark Horton of Bristol University presented to the attending masses at the town's manor court ceremony a story about Bideford's historic trading links with America. The presentation reignited my long-forgotten memories of those visits years previously to the British Museum. I subsequently spent much of the following buffet bombarding Professor Horton with questions about the events surrounding the Lost Colony and discussing the finer details of Bideford's involvement in this attempted founding of the New World.

Fired up by this sequence of events, I simply had to volunteer to take part in the much-planned 'Twinning Fact-Finding' mission to Manteo, under the leadership of our Mayor of the day and colleague, Councillor David Ratcliff. Manteo had much to show us, but of particular interest to me were the site of the Lost Colony settlement and the museum of artefacts associated with it. Despite some strong reservations about the mound of earth their National Park Service referred to as 'Ralph Lane's Fort of

1585' (which is almost certainly an American Civil War impostor), I came away with an even stronger desire to know what became of those colonists and who they really were.

The most significant fact that I learned from Manteo was that Sir Richard Grenville, onetime Lord of the Manor of Bideford and almost exclusively known for being the subject of an Alfred, Lord Tennyson poem, had been pivotal in those colonisation attempts. Yet he, like the Lost Colony itself, remained uncelebrated and generally unknown outside the Eastern Seaboard of North Carolina. Just how involved Grenville had been in those extraordinary years of 1584 to 1590 I was later to find out while researching for this book.

I returned to England committed to contacting a research group studying the events of that period. I found they exist, but only in America, and even then, at least one served only as a front for a charlatan who has seemingly evaded the law for years! Thanks, however, to our new connections with Manteo, I was soon in contact with Anne Poole and subsequently Roberta Estes, whose more professional group had dedicated itself to finding out who those colonists were and what happened to them. This group, I must add, operates on a purely voluntary basis.

In May 2009, I became Mayor of Bideford, which gave me the opportunity to raise the profile of the research the group was carrying out, with the intent of galvanising a similar project here in England. DNA testing, the core direction of Roberta's group, is and remains, though, a taboo subject in England. It is fraught with much bad press and public paranoia. It was therefore obvious that convincing people to offer their DNA for the project, even given that some limited funding to cover costs of these tests was available, was going to be an uphill struggle.

In a fit of stalemate, I turned my attention to taking a look at the historical evidence about the Lost Colony, in an attempt to understand the events of its disappearance more fully. What I found was that the entire saga of Raleigh's efforts to settle a colony in Virginia had been recorded with meticulous detail by Richard Hakluyt, an Elizabethan historian who had been commanded to record what we now term the Golden Age of Exploration during Queen Elizabeth's reign. Further research also revealed fragments of additional information from a surprising range of other sources, not least of those being the Spanish archives, much of which had never been studied in conjunction with Hakluyt's accounts.

It took some time for me to realise, too, that there had been only one serious attempt to interpret any of the known records of the period and compile them into a modern narrative of what happened during those fateful years between 1584 and 1590. The resultant book (Quinn, David B., *The Roanoke Voyages, 1584-1590* – See Reference 1) was published in the 1950s and was now at least fifty years old. Furthermore, in the time since its publication, much of its content has been called into question. There was obviously an opportunity to take a fresh look at the story.

In tracking down reliable sources of Hakluyt's records and those of others, I stumbled upon a first edition of Richard Hakluyt's *The Principall Navigations, Voiages, and Discoveries of the English Nation …(imprinted at London by George Bishop and Ralph Newberrie, Deputies to Christopher Baker, Printer to the Queen's Most Excellent Majesty)*. The book was published in 1589. It was an edition that surprised me with its subtle differences from the later amended and perhaps sanitised or politically corrected versions, many of which are so more readily available.

Given such a rare opportunity, I found myself compelled to transcribe the entire section about Roanoke into modern English, all this originally for my own research. Of course, this edition did not contain the later voyage of 1590, which I found first written about in the expanded version Richard Hakluyt published between 1598 and 1600 *(Third Volume, imprinted at London by George Bishop, Ralph Newberrie and Robert Baker 1600)*.

Having transcribed Hakluyt's accounts, I began to wonder about the principal characters mentioned in the texts, not least a certain Sir Richard Grenville. I found him to be a complex man who no doubt had a temper if matters did not go his way. But he was also intelligent, focussed on the tasks before him, and above all dedicated to his queen, his country and his people. Indeed, among many myths I dearly wish to dispel is that I believe he was never really appropriately labelled as a pirate. He was certainly never as ruthless as Drake or Hawkins, and whatever his privateering actions were, they were not enough for him to be held in anything but the highest regard in Queen Elizabeth's court. He was also a man of perhaps surprising compassion, who regularly displayed a responsibility for those who served under him. His adopted hometown of Bideford was never far from his heart, either. It is sad to record that his moment of fame occurred at his death, when in life he had clearly done so much more. Given his extraordinary commitment to Roanoke, it seems fitting to title this book to his credit and spend some time exploring his much unsung life. I have chosen therefore to preface these transcriptions with a short biography of his life.

My research also concluded that there was a need to resolve the confusing references to many of the locations associated with the story. Thanks to the useful but ethereal presence that is the internet, I was able to examine a plethora of early maps and studies of the area. The results of my examinations are contained in this book.

Rather surprisingly, during my research I discovered sources giving more information about the story in the form of remarkable eyewitness accounts, several of which provided alternative, sometimes complementary and sometimes conflicting viewpoints of the events surrounding the colony and the associated voyages. None of these accounts appear to have been known to Hakluyt, or if so, they were not thought relevant enough for him to include them. These, too, therefore had to be included in this book, if only to furnish as complete a picture as I believe can be made.

This book therefore is a compilation of those

transcriptions and associated research. However, given the obsession this story has become in my life, I have also included my own theories and text notes, all drawn exclusively from my own extensive research. My hope is that what you are about to read will at least provide a fresh, untainted and perhaps alternative perspective on these most extraordinary events.

Finally, if this book has any purpose beyond being what I hope will be a good read, it is perhaps to open the eyes of the English, who know so little of this extraordinary period in their history. It may also help to revise the views of Americans, who have had to endure so many rewrites by authors requoting David Beers Quinn. Perhaps most of all, though, I hope it will awaken a small town in the rural West Country of England to the realisation that it may yet prove to be the home of many of the founding fathers of America and that it IS home to one of the greatest unsung heroes of English History, Sir Richard Grenville.

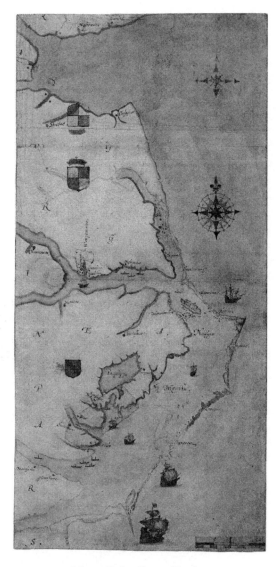

Map of the Outer Banks

Chapter One

~

A Short Biography of Sir Richard Grenville

It seems prudent to include a short biography of Sir Richard Grenville for when we look in detail at the events surrounding the Roanoke Colony we find his name inseparable from almost the entire saga. His involvement in leading the 1585 military colony is well documented, but what is less well known is his return barely a year later in 1586, when, with much puzzlement, he found the entire settlement of Roanoke deserted. Rather than just leaving, he spent some time looking for the expected military colony he had left behind the previous year, but failed to find it. Undaunted, he eventually committed some of his own men to holding the country for his queen and his partner in the venture, Sir Walter Raleigh, while he returned to England to report his findings; he was of course oblivious to the fact that Sir Francis Drake had evacuated the military colony barely two weeks before his arrival! In leaving his men at Roanoke he knew that even with a speedy resupply from England, they had to fend for themselves for at least six months or more. From what we now know of Grenville there should be no doubt that that decision could not have been easy.

In 1587, the year of the fateful voyage of the Lost Colony, there is almost no record of Grenville's involvement. The clue to his whereabouts can be found in the state calendar of Queen Elizabeth I, for she charged him on March 6th of that year to review the defences of both Devon and Cornwall in preparation for the expected war with Spain, something a lesser mortal might have taken years to complete, but which Grenville polished off in less than twelve months. Yet, despite this onerous task he still managed to meet Raleigh in London early in 1587 to drum up interest and agree on whom they should send to settle Roanoke.

In 1588, Grenville was quickly pressed into service by Raleigh again to prepare a substantial resupplying voyage to Roanoke. The ships were prepared at Bideford. Given the number and size of the ships involved (at least three of which were his own), this was some undertaking. There should be little doubt, too, that when this voyage was thwarted by the untimely arrival of the Spanish Armada, it was he who still found time to rustle up a couple of ships for the appointed governor of Roanoke (John White) later that same year. Thus, except for the exploratory voyage of 1584 and the final, ill-conceived voyage of 1590, almost everything else that happened in support of the Roanoke colonisation attempts happened because of one man: Sir Richard Grenville.

Given his intrinsic involvement in the subject of this book, it seems fitting to examine the life and times of Sir Richard in a little more detail.

To begin with, it has been widely recorded that he was considered irrational, tyrannical and overbearing by his peers. Ralph Lane, in his letters from Roanoke (See pages 61-65), for example, described Grenville as having 'intolerable pride' and 'insatiable ambition'. Yet Lane was involved in a bitter legal feud with Grenville, so at best it was surely in his interest to denigrate his General. We also read from various accounts of his dining habit of 'crashing the glass between his teeth until the blood ran from his mouth'. Since Grenville was an intelligent man, is it not more likely that this display was little more than his way of gaining enjoyment from the reaction of others? A party trick for the more boring and staid events and functions he attended, perhaps? Perhaps because of these sometimes erroneous or prejudiced accounts, his contribution to our nation and to the people who continue to benefit from his efforts today has been almost completely overlooked. It is sad to reflect that he has remained unrecognised in favour of those who, it could be argued with some justification, simple stole the credit for his ideas and efforts. Perhaps there is even justification enough to conclude that some of these same people may have written many of the adverse accounts of Sir Richard Grenville with the singular intent to deflect criticism away from their own failings.

Whatever his character, he was without doubt a man with an incessant drive, dedication and commitment to his queen, his country and to the people of his estates. Not least among these estates was the town of Bideford, a town intrinsically linked with the Grenvilles for almost six hundred years and where Sir Richard chose to make his family home.

So what of the Grenville family history? We know that they first arrived in Bideford as Lords of the Manor in 1126 after Henry I granted them title to the land on which the town and its strategically important ford sat. Yet apart from the charter Sir Richard de Greyvile (note the spelling of the last name) obtained for Bideford in May 1272, and the lobbying of the Bishops of Exeter to help finance and build Bideford's famous Long Bridge, not much is known of their early tenure. We have only fragments of information and occasional monuments and records to the family such as that in Bideford's parish church. We do not even know where they made their home before the building of Stowe House near Kilkhampton, a place our Sir Richard considered drafty and miserable in its location. Indeed, few realise that it is conceivable the Grenvilles had a house in Bideford long before the arrival of Sir Richard in 1542, for in building his own home there, Sir Richard referred to it as the family's 'new place at Bideford'. Was there indeed an 'old place' that remains undiscovered today?

Whatever the early history of the Grenvilles, it seems they chose to live in relative peace and obscurity. Relative obscurity, that is, until the arrival of our Sir Richard.

The exact date of birth of Sir Richard Grenville has been the subject of much debate, with dates commonly quoted between 1540 and 1543. The truth is that he was born in 1542. We know this from the existence of a portrait of him which hangs in the National Portrait Gallery, a copy of which also hangs half-hidden in Bideford's town council chambers. On that painting is the inscription '*AN. DNI. 1571. AETATIS. SUAE. 29*', which translates as '1571 A.D. in his age 29', meaning Grenville was twenty-nine years old in 1571.

We can even be specific about the precise date of birth in 1542 because of the tragedy that struck his father, Sir Roger Grenville, when Sir Richard was just three years old. Sir Roger was captain of King Henry VIII's flagship, the *Mary Rose,* which sank in extraordinary circumstances at Portsmouth in 1545 and whose remains are preserved in that city. At Sir Roger's post-mortem, his son, Sir Richard, is mentioned as having been born on June 5th. However, since this was in a time when the Julian calendar was in use, the date we should celebrate today under the modern, or Gregorian, calendar is ten days later, on 15 June 1542 [*Chancery Series 11, Vol 90, No 12*].

What remains a mystery about his birth is precisely where Sir Richard Grenville was born, for there are no parish records of his birth or christening, or at least none that have yet been found. However, given the presence of his grandfather's monument in the parish church of St Mary's, Bideford would appear to have a reasonable case for claiming to be that birthplace. Frustratingly, though, Richard was born nineteen years before records began in the parish. Thus, we can only conjecture whether Bideford truly has that right.

Sir Richard then disappears into obscurity for the next seventeen years. It is thought that he was raised at Clifton Arundell House on the Cornish side of the River Tamar, as a ward of court following the death of his father (there is a probable record of his minority in the Court of Wards). This location would make sense on account of his mother remarrying to Thomas Arundell following the tragic death of Richard's father.

Sir Richard finally resurfaces in 1559 when, evidently an intelligent lad, he was admitted to the Inner Temple of London to study at the tender age of seventeen. We should record that while the Inner Temple is associated with English law today, in Elizabethan times it was also a place where the landed gentry sent their heirs to be schooled. A year later Richard finally came of age and was granted his estates.

In 1562 we have the first inkling of a possibly volatile temper when we find that Richard (hereinafter 'Grenville') was involved in an 'Act of Affray' on 19 November 1562 which resulted in the death of his antagonist. The incident took place near St Clement Dane church in London. What the argument was about we do not know but there were several witnesses on both sides; one, Thomas Allen, a yeoman of the deceased, Roger Bannester, reported that Grenville had killed him by, (and I quote), 'running him throughe wit his sworde'. Even back in the gory days of Elizabethan England, such actions could readily have resulted in the death penalty being imposed for such a crime. Yet, whether by having the right connections or simply perhaps for being highly regarded in his studies, Grenville was pardoned for his rash actions, albeit after a discreet period in hiding [*Patent Rolls 29th year of Elizabeth 989*].

The following year, at just twenty-one years of age, Grenville was returned as Member of Parliament for Dunheved, Launceston. He remained in office, serving various constituencies in Cornwall in all three parliaments called before his death in 1591 [*Official return of Members of Parliament January 1st 1563*].

In 1565, Grenville married Mary St Leger, the daughter of John St Leger of Annery, Weare Giffard, a house and family long disappeared from our heritage. The St Legers were longtime friends of the Grenvilles, being their next door neighbours. The location of the marriage is, however, unknown. Grenville was not a stay-at-home, though, and there is some evidence that he went off to fight the Turks in Hungary barely a year after being married!

Of his wife, Mary, we do know she was an equal match for Grenville, for she managed to avoid capture when faced with an Irish uprising at Waterford and Cork in 1569, shortly after Grenville had left for England to obtain reinforcements. Indeed it is very likely Grenville knew the risks she faced at the time of his departure, and must have considered her capable of dealing with whatever befell her. When her husband was killed on board the *Revenge* at Flores in 1591, she was allowed to remain in their home on the quayside at Bideford unless she remarried. She died aged about 80 on 5 November 1623 having remained a widow for some thirty-two years. She is buried in St Mary's Parish Church, Bideford, alas without any known grave marker.

Regarding the Grenville family house at Bideford, it seems they began building it around the early 1580s. The exact location of the house at Bideford though has long remained a mystery and may have only recently been discovered by the author and Professor Mark Horton of Bristol University. At the time of writing, tests are being arranged to confirm the discovery of what is thought to be the last remaining fragment of it. The building in question was probably restructured in 1626, shortly after Mary's death. It is thought likely that the fragment that remains today was the part in which she spent her last days. The rest of what was once a substantial manor house was probably dismantled or simply pulled down during that restructuring. This hypothesis may explain why a number of rather incongruous features exist in the fabric of several other buildings in the town of Bideford today, many of which may lay claim to having once been part of the Grenville's 'new place at Bideford'.

When discussing the Grenvilles and their houses, it is worth recording something that is not widely recognised, perhaps thanks to a largely partisan marketing strategy: that the Grenvilles owned Buckland Abbey, a location so intrinsically linked with Sir Francis Drake, yet a house that the Grenvilles owned for nearly forty years. Indeed, what you see there today owes its existence and splendour almost exclusively to the efforts of Sir Richard Grenville and his grandfather.

It was Sir Richard Grenville's grandfather who was granted the abbey in 1541 for his support of the dissolution of the monasteries. He and his grandson were to spend a substantial sum of money rebuilding and remodelling the abbey. Our Grenville referred to it as his 'castle of comfort'. Exactly how much time he spent there is unknown but it was certainly long enough for his first children to be baptised at the church of nearby Buckland Monachorum.

Quite why Sir Richard Grenville sold it is open to conjecture, but given its proximity to Plymouth and Sir Francis Drake (someone whom, although related, Grenville had every reason to despise) he probably lost interest in the area and thus eventually sold it. The disposal was recorded as being to a Christopher Harris for £3,400 in

1580, who sold it barely six months later to Sir Francis Drake. It is not unreasonable to believe that Mr Harris was no more than an intermediary between Grenville and Drake [*Patent Roll Elizabeth 1209; 1580*].

With his marriage, Richard was drawn into the affairs of the province of Munster, the area centred on County Cork in Southern Ireland as it is today. The grandfather of his wife was Warham St Leger, to whom Queen Elizabeth I owed much for his suppression of the Irish warlords and for the settlement there of the English Protestant colonies. In 1569 Grenville took up joint ownership of the Kerrycurrihy estate in Munster with his father-in-law, John St Leger. It was the first of numerous acquisitions Grenville was to make in Southern Ireland.

However, Sir Richard's interests in the town of Bideford were never far from his mind. The area had, according to records of the time, become run-down, with the market and associated fair largely having ceased to take place. If Bideford was to be the home of the Grenvilles, then as Lords of the Manor, this was clearly an unacceptable state of affairs. In 1572, three hundred years after his ancestors secured the first charter, Sir Richard obtained a new charter for the town; whether this was a deliberate tercentennial act of celebration we do not know. What is certain is the new charter, whilst making great play on the structure of the town's governing body of aldermen and burghers, their powers, and the resurrection of the market and fair, also recognised Bideford as a port. It seems certain Grenville had the vision to recognise the value this latter asset would have for the town [*Chancery Warrants File 1268*].

To get such sweeping powers for the new governing body, however, Grenville would have had to obtain consent from the local landowners, and to do so he would have been obliged to ensure that their powers remained reasonably intact. Since Grenville was the principal exponent of the charter, the town's Lord of the Manor, and a Member of Parliament, we can be absolutely certain that Grenville would have elected himself as an alderman of the borough. He would therefore have voted for Bideford's first Mayor, John Salterne, a man whom history records as a merchant adventurer. Electing someone with a vested interest in shipping and trade would have been an ideal choice for Grenville's plans for Bideford.

The legacy of Grenville's acts remains with Bideford today. The Grenville coat of arms forms part of the town's coat of arms, and the council retains an Elizabethan mace complete with the Grenville coat of arms on it. It is not unrealistic to think that this symbol of office was paid for and presented to the town by Grenville himself.

Grenville also secured a covenant, dated 4 September 1575, which granted his family the revenues, issues and profits within the manor of Bideford 'excepting fee-farm rent of 10s 6d per annum and the office of Port reeve'. As an aside, one wonders today when the office of the Port reeve was finally dissolved. Nevertheless, in return for this grant the Grenvilles gave the town various rights including the 'use of the chapel standing at the west end of the bridge and ground whereof certain limekilns sometime stood, and where a quay, or wharf, is now lately builded' [*Earl Grafton Private Papers 1575*].

Grenville was often in London on parliamentary or

court duties, or simply meeting with Raleigh and others. Exactly where he lived while in London, like much of his life, has always been something of a mystery. However, documents in the State Papers make it clear that he lived at the St Leger's house, near St Olave in Southwark. It was formerly the house of the abbot of St Augustine's, Canterbury. In John Stow's *Survey of London* (1598), its location was described as being next to a stone yard that repaired the Southwark Bridge.

Perhaps the greatest 'if only' moment of Grenville's life came on 22 March 1574. On this date he presented a petition to the Elizabethan court to seek approval for a voyage to find the South Sea (the Pacific Ocean), a project for which Grenville had already purchased a ship, the *Castle of Comfort,* at Plymouth four years earlier. In the acts of the Privy Council and records from the High Court of the Admiralty we know that Grenville stated the voyage would serve not only to find a shorter trading route to the Spice Islands of the East Indies but would also thwart Spanish expansion plans in South America. The *Castle of Comfort* was well known as a notorious fighting ship, regularly appearing in the State Papers ('never once found in peaceful trade', to quote one reference). This fact, coupled with the belief that a delicate but workable relationship still existed with Spain, probably led the court to consider that approving the voyage might not be prudent at the time. Thus Grenville's petition was turned down.

Perhaps the only recognition Grenville is ever likely to receive as originator of this idea over Sir Francis Drake can be summed up by three indisputable facts. First, Grenville's petition to Lord Burghley is endorsed 'Mr

Grenville's Voyage' and signed in Lord Burghley's own hand. Second, John Butler, pilot to John Oxenham during his exploits in the West Indies and Central America, issued a deposition (dated 20 February 1579) to the Spanish authorities while captive in Lima, Peru, which referenced Grenville's intentions to plot a South Sea voyage. And finally, three years later Drake, who would unquestionably have known and had access to Grenville's work, set out to follow an almost identical course and to conduct remarkably similar actions against the Spanish as no doubt Grenville intended. We can therefore be sure that if Grenville had been given consent back in 1574 it would have been he and the *Castle of Comfort* and not Drake and the *Golden Hind* who would be so remembered for that now-fabled journey [*State Papers Domestic Elizabeth, 95 No. 63, 64 and 65*; *Acts of the Privy Council IX 111, 130, 132 ~ 1576; High Court of the Admiralty Vol 22, 19 July 1576; Lansdowne MSS No. 100 f.4.* also, *researched by Hakluyt Society and published in their 1914 volume, pages 1-12*].

Following this disappointment, Grenville, who received his knighthood the following October at Windsor Castle, spent much of the fund he had taken years to build up in preparation for his South Sea venture by expanding his property portfolio. Of particular interest are those purchases that enlarged his holdings at Bideford; these included the neighbouring manor of Lancras (Landcross) and the hamlet of Upcott Snelard (Upcott), the former being subject to much bitter legal dispute, which according to the Close Rolls of 18 May 1576, Grenville eventually won.

In 1577 Grenville became High Sheriff of Cornwall.

He also took possession of Lundy Island from John St Leger, which he at once began to fortify, perhaps in the expectation that a fight with the Spanish was unavoidable. Lundy's strategic importance was obviously not lost on Grenville, sitting as it does at the mouth of the Bristol Channel [*Close Rolls 20 Elizabeth part 1 (C54/1024*].

Over the next seven years we know that Grenville busied himself with his estates in Ireland, serving his country as a regular investigator into piracy, and in curtailing the practicing of the Roman Catholic faith. The latter was conducted with particular vengeance, most notably at Launceston, Cornwall.

By 1585, had it not been for the insistence of Queen Elizabeth that Raleigh should stay in England to be at her side, we can be certain that Grenville would have spent his days pottering around the West Country in relative obscurity. Instead, while he was obliged to play to the Queen's affections, Raleigh sent for cousin Grenville to lead the military colony to Roanoke.

Exactly how Grenville tackled the venture can best be described as planned to the utmost degree and done so with single-minded determination. We should remember that the voyage to the New World was his first recorded venture onto the high seas. Given the enormity of the task and the risks he faced, Grenville first placed his estates into the hands of trustees in case of his death. Tragically, through the short-sightedness of a Victorian town clerk, this document now missing is thought to have gone into the bonfire along with over two hundred years of Grenville records believed to have been in the hands of the then Bideford borough council.

Grenville's reward for his efforts at Roanoke in 1585 was a handsome Spanish prize he took near Bermuda on his return to England. This ship of some 300 tonnes, the *Santa Maria de Vincente*, was brought into Bideford and converted into the *Dudley*, a ship that was ironically later involved in the fight against the Spanish Armada.

There were two extraordinary consequences of capturing this ship. One, that in doing so Grenville took several Spaniards prisoner. One of these was Pedro Diaz, a Portuguese pilot who later escaped, ironically from John White's ill-fated 1588 voyage, and gave a deposition to the Spanish authorities of Havana four years after his original capture. In it he talks of being forced to build Grenville's house in Bideford and states that many of his companion Spaniards died during that time (one wonders where they were buried). The second extraordinary consequence is that the cannons from the Spanish ship would have been of a different gauge to English cannons and therefore largely useless. Is it just conceivable that these are the cannons found up-ended and half buried in the old Bideford quayside where they had evidently been used as mooring posts, which are now displayed as part of a Children's Fort in nearby Victoria Park and labelled as 'Spanish Armada' cannons?

One final note from Grenville's voyage to Roanoke in 1585 is to record that after Grenville arrived back at Plymouth, he was 'courteously received by diverse of his worshipful friends', among whom it seems was Raleigh, who 'did presently resolve upon another voyage, to supply Ralfe Lane and his company that were left with him in Virginia, the next Spring following' *[Plymouth Muniments Widey Court Book 1585]*.

In 1586 Grenville sailed from Bideford back to Roanoke with the same two ships he took the previous year (the *Roebuck* and *Tyger*) but found the island deserted. Elizabethan Historian Richard Hakluyt records that Grenville left fifteen of his own men to defend America for the Queen. Their names however, were not recorded by him, yet from the remarkable deposition by Pedro Diaz in 1589 we do at least know one was a Master Coffin and one a Chapman.

In 1587 Grenville spent time in both London and Bideford working on finding people for Raleigh's colony. Exactly whom he obtained we know thanks to Richard Hakluyt's list. Where they came from remains a mystery that is discussed in more detail later in this book.

In 1588 Grenville again attempted to supply the Roanoke colony but with his ships full of victuals he was thwarted by the Privy Council and directed to support the English fight against the Spanish Armada. In effect he had little choice but to second his intended Roanoke fleet and refit them for a fight with the Spanish.

Exactly how many ships were in the fleet that sailed from North Devon to fight the Spanish, and whose ships they were, has been the subject of much debate for perhaps a century or more, but after much research by the author, the list that follows is probably as accurate as can be hoped for:

Dudley ~ weighing about 300 tonnes and owned by Grenville; this was the Spanish prize *Santa Maria de Vincente* of 1585. It was captained by James Erisey (sometimes spelled Erizoy). It had a contingent of a hundred men. Of note is that James Erisey was captain of the *White Lion* during Drake's West Indian voyage of 1586, which evacuated Ralph Lane's military colony from Roanoke.

Virgin God Save Her ~ weighing around 200 tonnes, and owned by Grenville. Its captain was Sir Richard's second son, John, who was very much a chip off the old block but whose promising career was tragically cut short when he died later in 1595 while captaining one of Raleigh's ships on his voyage to Guyana. She carried eighty men to fight the Spanish.

Tyger ~ weighing between 140 and 200 tonnes and owned by Grenville; this was of course Grenville's flagship, captained by James Bostock. She carried a hundred men.

Golden Hind ~ described as a pinnace of some 50 tonnes. She was captained by Thomas Fleming and played a brave role in the fight against the Spanish Armada by serving as the English fleet's lookout. She was successful and can claim to be the first English ship to bring news of the Spanish Armada to England. She carried fifty men. There remains a curious tale regarding this ship, involving Sir Francis Drake, who apparently objected to her name being that of his own *Golden Hind* of round-the-world fame. As a result she was renamed *Bark Fleming* after her captain, and this is how she appears on tapestries depicting the battle.

Bark St Leger ~ weighing around 50 tonnes and owned by the St Legers. She was captained by John St Leger's son (also called John). Oddly she does not appear in the records associated with the battle with the Spanish Armada, There remains a possibility she was sent instead to Ireland under Grenville's direction.

[Sources for the above information include *The Tapestry Hangings of the House of Lords Representing the several Engagements between the English and Spanish fleets in the ever memorable Year MDLXXXVIII Author John Pine (Engraver) Published 1739; amongst others.*]

We also know that Grenville had at least two other ships prepared in that flotilla but they never sailed for Plymouth. It is thought they were left behind because he had been given the authority to take only those he thought capable of a good fight. The names of those two ships are officially not known, but they might just be the *Brave* and the *Roe*, the two ships that formed John White's ill-fated attempt to reach Virginia later that year.

The exact port of origin of the fleet that sailed from North Devon to battle with the Spanish Armada has also been subjected to another battle: that of ownership between Bideford and its ancient neighbour Barnstaple, but this, too, can be resolved by a record of the Privy Council. In it, Barnstaple pleads poverty to the Queen's Privy Council when asked to raise support for the defence of the realm. What part Barnstaple took in that glorious fight was ultimately thanks to two privateers, the *Bark Sellinger* of 50 tonnes, captained by its owner, John Sellinger, and the *John of Barnstaple* of some 40 tonnes whose captain remains unknown. It is therefore indisputable that the fleet that sailed to fight the Spanish Armada set sail from the quayside of Bideford and it was Grenville that led them to Plymouth.

Having delivered his fleet, Grenville did not take part in the fight against the Spanish Armada; exactly why not is now known thanks to the discovery of two crucial pieces of information. First, a fragment of a note that records a John Hender of Launceston being asked (and paid 1/- for the task) 'to run to Bideford with post letters to Sir Richard Grenville that came from Sessions' which confirms Grenville was in Bideford a mere five days before John White sailed from there for Roanoke with the *Brave* and the *Roe* [*Blanchminster's Charity* ~ *page 73 and others*]. The second fragment is in the deposition of Pedro Diaz, in which he reports in context with Roanoke that 'the commander made ready two small vessels'. This, Diaz states, occurred in 1588. It can only be a reference to White's voyage from Bideford; the 'commander' being Grenville.

Grenville wasn't to miss all the fighting against the Spanish though. His chance came when, on September 14th later that year, he was formally commanded by Queen Elizabeth to undertake the defence of the western approaches following news that the Spanish Armada was steadily making its way around Scotland and the west coast of Ireland. The precise wording of that command reads, 'We have thought meet to make choice of you for this service'. The command follows with details to guard the Severn (the Bristol Channel) and fortify Waterford and Cork. Sadly for Grenville, his chance of fame was dashed on the rocks of the west coast of Ireland. For his pains in supplying ships and men for the battle against the Spanish

Armada, though, his financial receipt from Lord Howard and Sir John Hawkins was £1960 for providing seven hundred men for four months, and for providing his ships totalling 800 tonnes, he earned £320 [*Acts of Privy Council 1588 277; State Papers Domestic Elizabeth 216 no 54, 237, f 15*].

Between October 1588 and 1590 Grenville turned his attentions back to his plantations in Munster, a project he had first been involved with twenty years earlier. Queen Elizabeth's government wanted 'gentlemen of substance' to undertake to settle and repopulate the area with Protestants. Grenville duly obliged. By May 1589 Grenville had settled ninety-nine English in Munster, including his son John Grenville, his half-brother John Arundell, Christopher Harris of Radford (near Plymouth), Thomas Stukeley, John Facey, John Bellew and many others.

He also extended his estates to include Gilly (later St Finbar's Monastery), lands at Kilmoney and Kinalmeaky, and Fermoy Abbey, which was leased to the Grenvilles for forty years. Sadly, the legal conclusion of these purchases and leases was never seen by Grenville for when they were sealed, he was already in the Azores on his last fateful journey for his country [*State Papers Ireland 133 no 85, 142 no 53; Calendar Patent and Close Rolls Ireland 11, 195 & 201 June 1591*].

We now come to the fateful year of 1591. As part of a plan to strangle Spain's trade with its West Indian empire, England decided to blockade the Azores. Grenville was appointed vice admiral of the *Revenge*, one of Lord Howard's ships, which was owned by the queen. It was regarded as one of the finest in the fleet, recognition surely of Grenville's skills as a sea captain.

What happened during that fateful event has largely always been thought to follow closely Raleigh's report on the Battle of Flores, but we know now that this report was inaccurate. The evidence for this comes from two remarkable sources: a first-hand Spanish account from on board Don Alonso de Bazan's flagship, and testimony from the 50-tonne *Foresight* (the only ship that came back to help the *Revenge,* which, after two hours, had little choice but to flee or be taken). There are also other sources that add subtle detail to what took place.

From the start, the Spanish fleet knew the English were at anchor on the northward side of the island of Flores and thus decided to split into two flotillas and circumnavigate the island to catch the English in a pincer movement. On sight of the Spanish, Lord Howard, having been caught unawares, fled with his fleet, leaving the *Revenge* and Grenville to fend for themselves.

Accounts state the English fleet had left many men on the island of Flores, some to seek water and others to gain some respite from a sickness that had swept through the fleet. In Sir Richard Hawkins' book *Observations* (See Reference 2) he records that 'Grenville would not leave his men ashore for the Spanish to take'. This almost certainly explains why he was the last to leave. Despite various comments about Grenville's personality he was clearly a man loyal to his men.

Grenville and the *Revenge* each had a great deal of 'previous history' with the Spanish fleet, and with Lord Howard already a long chase away, records suggest the Spanish saw the capture of both Grenville and the *Revenge* as the best possible prize from their action against the

English. The Spanish records on Grenville state: 'Almirante Ricardo de Campo Verde gran corsario y de mucha estimacion entrellos' (Admiral Richard Grenville, a great corsair and of great estimation among them). And the record on the *Revenge* after she was finally taken states, 'This Admiral Galleon was one of the best there were in England; they called her the Revenge. She was the flagship that carried Drake to Corunna'.

The first attempt to take the *Revenge* came from the *San Felipe,* which boarded her with nine or ten soldiers. In the following hand-to-hand combat, seven of them were killed. The ships then broke free. Aramburu's flagship then tried boarding the *Revenge*, but was repelled and, according to the Spaniard's own admission, badly damaged in the engagement. It was then the turn of the *Ascencion* under Don Antonio Manrique to try to board the *Revenge* but she, too, was beaten off.

The Spanish account goes on to state that the *Revenge* became unrigged and dismasted but was still fighting. She continued to fight and in the continuing battle sent both Vice Admiral Luis Cuitinho's ship, the *La Serena,* and the *Ascencion* to the bottom of the sea. These accounts also record that several other ships in their fleet were badly damaged in the engagement.

Grenville was wounded in the head by a musket shot just before midnight. A great many accounts claim this was fired from one of his own men. This is nonsense; after all, Grenville had stayed loyal to his men throughout the ill-fated voyage, and from his many previous voyages and exploits in the West Indies and Roanoke, there is not a single account of mutiny. In fact, the first inkling we ever have of his men rebelling does not come until the following daybreak at Flores, when we find the *Revenge* almost out of powder, having no pikes left to repel boarders, and its decks littered with the bodies of forty men. The ship was also slowly sinking from a catalogue of cannon and artillery shot.

It is at this point in the fight that Grenville is recorded by the subsequently repatriated mariners as commanding his men to arrange for the ship to be split asunder and sunk so she would not be taken. The crew said no, probably because they hoped to save themselves by handing over the *Revenge* to the Spanish as the prize they so dearly wanted. With his crew not prepared to sink the ship and having nothing left to fight with, Grenville had no choice but to surrender.

By now, Grenville's injuries must have started to tell on him and it is clear from what followed that he was resigned to undergoing whatever the Spanish had in store for him, probably knowing he was either going to die under torture or from his wounds in any event. According to the Spanish records what they did was take him onboard the *San Pedro*, none other than the Spanish flagship. There they dressed his multiple wounds and gave him a meal of his choosing.

The Spanish account states that while Grenville sat at the table, 'Don Alonso would not see him yet all the rest of the captains and gentlemen did visit him to comfort him and to wonder at his courage and stout heart, for that he showed not any sign of faintness nor changing of colour.'

Sometime after Grenville's death, the Spanish admiral, Don Alonso, wrote, 'El Almirante de los mayors marineros y cosarios de inglaterra gran hereje y perseguidor de catholicos' (The admiral of the master mariners and corsairs of England [was] a great heretic and persecutor of the Catholics). He added, 'Mas la herida era grande y murio otro dia' (But his wound was grievous and in a day or two he died).

Grenville was buried at sea on the way to Terceira. The *Revenge* also sank en route. Some accounts state that the *Revenge* was left to dash against the cliffs of Terceira, but this is not recorded in the Spanish records.

The Spanish quoted their official losses as a hundred men and two captains; only two ships were declared lost, but many were subtly noted as having been severely damaged.

English accounts suggest that up to fifty-three ships were involved but this, too, is incorrect. There may have been many more ships in the Spanish fleet as a number did not engage in Don Alonso's attack, but what is certain is that a total of twenty-nine ships in two flotillas (of eighteen ships and eleven ships each) attacked the *Revenge* in that pincer movement *[Coleccion Navarette XXV (Nos: 48, 49); A. de I., 54-1-34, Santo Domingo 1 18. 1 pliego, Cf. Document No. 10, ante]*.

The events surrounding the Battle of Flores had a consequence that rippled around the Atlantic and through the Spanish Empire for many years afterwards. The single-handed battle Grenville had fought not only severely hampered their expansion plans but also provided sufficient delay to the arrival of their treasure ships from the West Indies that they were caught in the worst storms for a century. Spanish maritime power never recovered.

In his book *Considerations Touching a War with Spain,* (Imprinted 1629) Francis Bacon described Grenville's actions as 'that memorable fight of an English ship called the *Revenge,* memorable I say even beyond credit, and to the height of some heroic fable'. As fitting an epitaph as this extraordinary statement is, I believe it perhaps equally fitting to close this short and by no means complete biography with the prophetic words of Sir Richard's Grandfather:

Who seeks the way to win renown,
Or flies with wings of high desire
Who seeks to wear the laurel crown,
Or hath the mind that would aspire:
Let him his native soil eschew,
Let him go range and seek anew

To pass the seas some think a toil,
Some think it strange abroad to roam;
Some think it grief to leave their soil,
Their parents, kinfolks, and their home.
Think so who list, I like it not
I must abroad to try my lot.

Who lists at home at cart to drudge
And cark and care for worldly trash,
With buckled shoes let him go trudge,
Instead of lance or whip to slash:
A mind that base his kind will show
Of carrion sweet to feed a crow.

If Jason of that mind had been
The Grecians when they came to Troy
Had never so the Trojans fought,
Nor never put them to such annoy:
Wherefore who list to live at home.
To purchase fame I will go roam.

(taken from '*Grenville*' A L Rowse 1936 – See Reference 3.)

Sir Richard Grenville

The Transcriptions

(with text notes by the author)

Chapter Two

~

The Voyage of Amadas and Barlowe 1584

The following is a transcript of the original Hakluyt records compiled in 1589. It records the first voyage to find a place for the English to settle a colony on American soil.

The first voyage made to the coast of America, with two Barkes, wherein were Captains Master Philip Amadas and Master Arthur Barlowe, who discovered part of the country, now called Virginia, Anno 1584: Written by one of the said Captains, and sent to Sir Walter Raleigh, Knight, at whose charge, and direction, the said voyage was set forth.

The 27th, day of April in the year of our redemption, 1584, we departed the west of England [1] with two barkes, well favoured with men and victuals, having received our last and perfect directions by your letters, confirming the former instructions, and commandments delivered by yourself at our leaving the river of Thames [2] And I think

[1] Some later versions give the specific departure port as Plymouth.
[2] 'Leaving the river of Thames' is not recorded in some later versions; clearly Amadas and Barlowe must have visited Raleigh at his London home (Durham House) to receive instructions (as stated) and from there presumably sailed to a West Country port to prepare and set sail for Virginia.

it a matter both unnecessary, for the manifest discovery of the country, as also for tediousness sake, to remember unto you the diurnall [3] of our course, sailing thither, and returning : only I have presumed to present unto you this brief discourse, by which you may judge how profitable this land is likely to succeed, as well to your self (by whole direction and charge, and by whole servants this our discovery hath been performed) as also to her highness, and the commonwealth, in which we hope your wisdom will be satisfied, considering, that as much by us hath been brought to light, as by those small means, and number of men we had, could any way have been expected or hoped for. [3a]

* * *

The tenth of May we arrived at the Canaries, and the tenth of June in this present piece, we were fallen with the islands of the West Indies, keeping a more south-easterly course then was needful, because we doubted that the current of the bay of Mexico, disbogging [4] between the Cape of Florida and the Havana, had been of greater force then afterwards we found it to be.

At which islands we found the air very unwholesome, and our men grieve for the most part ill disposed: so that having refreshed ourselves with sweet water, and fresh

[3] 'Diurnall' ~ a cross between a journal and a diary; it is a term that has fallen into disuse.
[3a] A fawning and awkward few sentences, perhaps saying 'We hope you're satisfied with what we did!'
[4] 'Disbogging' ~ possibly meaning 'disembogue', to come out of the mouth of a river; in context perhaps meaning 'discharging'.

victual, we departed the twelfth day after our arrival there. These islands, with the rest adjoining, are so well known to yourself, and to many others, as I will not trouble you, with the remembrance of them.

The second of July, we found shoal water, which smelt so sweetly, and was so strong a smell, as if we had been in the midst of some delicate garden, abounding with all kinds of odiferous flowers, by which we were assured, that the land could not be far distant: and keeping good watch, and bearing but slack sail, the fourth of the same month, we arrived upon the coast, which we supposed to be a continent, and firm land, [4a] and we sailed along the same, a hundred and twenty English miles, before we could find any entrance, or river, issuing into the sea. [4b]

* * *

The first that appeared unto us, we entered, though not without some difficulty, and cast anchor about three

[4a] *It could be that Cape Lookout was the first sighting of the coast Amadas and Barlowe made, jutting out as it does from the general line of the south-eastern coast of America. It is unlikely that it was Cape Fear they identified as they would have had to remain invisible from the Spanish Florida shore to avoid interest and suspicion, especially since Spain and England were by now almost at war.*

N.B. Spanish Florida extended much further north than the American state of Florida does today. A map of Spanish Florida drawn by Heiron Chiaves in 1584 shows Port Royal, South Carolina, and the area around Georgetown as being within the Spanish domain. Jacques Le Moyne's 1591 map of the same area depicts Cape Fear ('Prom S. Romam') as the northern limit of Spanish territory.

[4b] *Once discovering the coast, Amadas and Barlowe continued to sail parallel to the coast but evidently remained some distance offshore as they clearly missed several of the more low-lying inlets in the '120 miles' they travelled before finally spotting one significantly visible enough to be noticed at their distance from shore.*

harquebushot [5] within the havens mouth, on the left hand of the same and after thanks given to God for our safe arrival thither, we manned our boats and went to view the land next adjoining [5a] and to take possession of the same, in the right of the Queen's most excellent majesty, as rightful Queen and Princess of the same, and after delivered the same over to your use, according to her majesty's grant, and letters patent, under her highnesses great seal.

* * *

Which being performed, according to the ceremonies used in such enterprises, we viewed the land about us, being whereas the first landed, very sandy, and low towards the water line, but so full of grapes, as the very beating, and surge of the sea overflowed them, of which we found such plenty, as well there, as in all places else, both on the land, and on the green soil on the hills, as in the plains, as well on every little shrub, as also climbing towards the tops of the high Cedars, that I think in all the world the like abundance is not to be found: and myself having seen those parts of Europe that most abound, find such difference, as were incredible to be written.

We passed from the seaside, towards the tops of the

[5] 'Harquebushot' ~ an arquebus (also harkbut) was an early matchlock rifle. The distance of one arquebus shot was based on its effective killing distance. This was approximately the same distance a good archer could kill someone with an arrow, or about one hundred yards. Thus they anchored roughly three hundred yards inside the inlet to the inner sea.

[5a] 'Land next adjoining' ~ a confusing expression, although as used in this context it could refer to the neighbouring island rather than the land near to which they moored.

hills next adjoining, being but of mean height, and from hence we beheld the sea on both sides to the north, and to the south, finding no end any of both ways. This land lay stretching itself to the west, which after we found to be but an island of twenty leagues [6] long, and not above five miles broad. Under the bank or hill, whereon we stood, we beheld the valleys replenished with goodly cedar trees, and having discharged our harquebushot, such a flock of cranes (the most part white) arose under us, with such a cry redoubled by many echoes, as if an army had shouted altogether. [6a]

* * *

This island had many goodly woods, and full of deer, conies, hares, and fowl, even in the middle of summer, [7]

---

[6] 'Leagues' ~ a league measured on land was roughly three miles; however, if discussed in nautical terms, as the author of this account, being a mariner, would have done, then a league would have measured around three and a half miles. Thus 'twenty leagues' could mean sixty or seventy miles. In this narrative that would place their mooring near the present-day Oregon Inlet, implying that they were, in fact, exploring Bodie Island. This assumes also that Cape Lookout was the first point of land they noted after leaving Spanish Florida. However, the 1600 edition has the words 'twenty leagues' replaced with 'twenty miles' and the comment 'The isle of Wokokon' inserted in the margin. If this correction by Hakluyt is accurate, then it seems that given the mileage Amadas and Barlowe quoted of 120 miles, they had in fact spotted Cape Fear further south and not Cape Lookout on July 4th and explored the area of what is today Ocracoke Village and not Bodie Island.
The later comment by Hakluyt has done much to confuse the precise location of their first landing.
[6a] The discharge of the harquebus (arquebus) did not arouse an immediate response from any natives. This fact and later notes in the account may confirm that Amadas and Barlowe were exploring unpopulated land. This adds to the theory that they may have been on or near Bodie Island.
[7] In England, waterfowl migration is usually driven by the winter season. In summer the coastal mudflats are almost empty, hence their obvious surprise at the sight before them.

in incredible abundance. The woods are not such as you find in Bohemia, [8] Moscovia, [9] or Hyrcania, [10] barren and fruitless, but the highest and reddest Cedars of the world, far bettering the Cedars of the Azores, of the India's or of Lybanus, [11] Pines, Cypress, Sassafras, the Lentisk or the tree that bears the Mastic, [11a] the tree that bears the rind of Black Cinnamon, of which Master Winter brought from the straights of Magellan, and many other of excellent smell, and quality.

* * *

We remained by the side of this island two whole days, before we saw any people of the country: the third day we espied one small boat rowing towards us, having in it three persons: this boat came to the lands side, four harquebushot from our ships, and there two of the people remaining, the third came along the shore side towards us, and we being then all within board, he walked up and down upon the point of the land next unto us: then the master and the pilot of the Admiral, Simon Ferdinando, and the Captain Philip Amadas, myself, [12] and others, rowed to the land whose coming this fellow attended, never making any show of fear, or doubt.

[8] *A reference in context to the Black Forest.*
[9] *Russia.*
[10] *The area to the south of the Caspian Sea.*
[11] *Lebanon.*
[11a] *'Lentisk' ~ the mastic tree, a member of the same genus as the pistachio.*
[12] *The 1600 edition states that the narrator was Captain Arthur Barlowe. In this 1589 version no one is credited. The use of 'myself' is the nearest term of reference we have to Captain Arthur Barlowe being the author of this account.*

* * *

And after he had spoken of many things not understood by us, we brought him with his own good liking, aboard the ships, and gave him a shirt, a hat, and some other things, and made him taste of our wine, and our meat, which he liked very well: and after having viewed both barks, he departed, and went to his own boat again, which he had left in a little cove, or creek adjoining: as soon as he was two bowshot [13] into the water, he fell to fishing, and in less than half an hour, he had laden his boat as deep, as it could swim, with which he came again to the point of the land, and there he divided his fish into two parts, pointing one part to the ship, and the other to the Pinesse: which after he had (as much as he might,) required the former benefits received, he departed out of our sight.

* * *

The next day there came unto us diverse boats and in one of them the Kings brother, accompanied with forty or fifty men, being handsome, and good people, and in their behaviour as mannerly and civil as any of Europe.

His name was Granganimeo, and the King is called Wingina, the country Wingandacoa, (and now by her majesty, Virginia,) [14] the manner of his coming was in

[13] 'Bowshot' ~ one bowshot is about one hundred yards, the same distance as a 'harquebushot'.
[14] The name Virginia for the country had therefore been predetermined by the English in honour of the Virgin Queen and was not influenced by the similarity of the native name 'Wingina', a commonly held theory. The name 'Wingandacoa' was later determined to mean the equivalent of 'You have nice clothes'!

this sort: he left his boats altogether, as the first man did, a little from the ships by the shore, and came along to the place over against the ships, followed with forty men.

When he came to the place, his servants spread a long mat upon the ground, on which he sat down, and at the other end of the mat, four others of his company did the like: the rest of his men stood round about him, somewhat a far off: when we came to the shore to him with our weapons, he never moved from his place, nor any of the other four, nor never mistrusted any harm to be offered from us, but sitting still, he beckoned us to come and sit by him, which we performed: and being set, he makes all signs of joy, and welcome, striking on his head, and his breast, and afterwards on ours, to show we were all one, smiling, and making show the best he could, of all love, and familiarity.

After he had made a long speech unto us, we presented him with diverse things, which he received very joyfully and thankfully. None of his company dared to speak one word all the time: only the four which were at the other end, spoke in one another's ear very softly.

The king is greatly obeyed, and his brothers, and children reverenced: the king himself in person was at our being there for wounded, in a fight which he had with the King of the next country, called Wingina, and was shot in two places through the body, and one clean through the thigh, but yet he recovered: by reason whereof, and for that he lay at the chief town of the Country, being five days journey off, we saw him not at all. After we had presented this his brother, with such things as we thought he liked, we likewise gave somewhat to the other that sat with him on the mat: but presently he arose, and took all from them, and put it into his own basket, making signs and tokens, that all things ought to be delivered unto him, and the rest were but his servants, and followers.

A day or two after this, we fell to trading with them, exchanging some things we had for Chamois, Buff, and deer skins: when we showed him all our packet of merchandise, of all things that he saw, a bright tin dish most please him, which he presently took up, and clasped it before his breast, and after made a hole in the brim thereof and hung it about his neck, making signs, that it would defend him against his enemies arrows: for those people maintain a deadly and terrible war, with the people and king adjoining.

We exchanged our tin dish for twenty skins, worth twenty crowns, or twenty nobles: and a copper kettle for fifty skins, worth fifty crowns. They offered us very good exchange for our hatchets, and axes, and for knives, and would have given anything for swords: but we would not depart with any.

After two or three days, the kings brother came aboard the ships, and drank wine, and ate of our meat, and of our bread, and liked exceedingly thereof: and after a few days overpassed, he brought his wife with him to the ships, his daughter, and two or three little children: his wife was very well favoured, of mean stature, and very bashfull: she had on her back a long cloak of leather, with the fur side next to her body, and before her a piece of the same: about her forehead, she had a broad band of white coral, [15] and so had her husband many times: in her ears she had bracelets

[15] *In the 1600 edition there is a margin note that qualifies this as 'white coral pearls'.*

37

of pearls, hanging down to her middle, (whereof we delivered your worship a little bracelet) [16] and those were of the bigness [17] of good peas.

* * *

The rest of her women of the better sort, had pendants of copper, hanging in every ear: and some of the children of the Kings brother, and other noblemen, have five or six in every ear: he himself had upon his head, a broad plate of gold or copper, for being unpolished, we knew not what metal it should be, neither would he by any means suffer us to take it off his head, but feeling it, it would have very easily. His apparel was as his wives, only the women wear their hair long on both sides, and the men but on one. They are of colour yellowish, and their hair black for the most, and yet we saw children that had very fine auburn and chestnut colour hair.

After that these women had been there, there came down from all parts great store of people, bringing with them leather, coral, diverse kinds of dyes very excellent, and exchanged with us: but when Granganimeo, the Kings brother was present, none durst [18] to trade but himself, except such as were red pieces of copper on their heads, like himself: for that is the difference between the noblemen, and Governors of Countries, and the meaner sort.

[16] *This implies that Raleigh was presented with a Croatoan pearl bracelet; no evidence of its existence is known today.*
[17] *'Of the bigness' ~ meaning 'of the size'.*
[18] *'Durst' ~ dared.*

And we both noted there, and you have understood since by these men, which we brought home [19] that no people in the world carry more respect to their king, Nobility, and Governors, than these do.

The king's brother's wife, when she came to us, as she did many times, she was followed with forty of fifty women always: and when she came into the ship, she left them all on land, saving her two daughters, her nurse, and one or two more.

The King's brother always kept this order, as many boats as he would come withal to the ships, so many fires would he make on the shore afar off, to the end we might understand with what strength, and company he approached. Their boats are made of one tree, either of pine, or of pitch trees: a wood not commonly known to our people, nor growing in England.

They have no edge tools to make them withal: if they have any, they are very few, and those it seems they had twenty years since, which as those two men declared, [20] was out of a wreck which happened upon their coast of some Christian ship, being beaten that way by some storm, and outrageous weather, whereof none of the people were saved, but only the ship, or some part of her, being cast upon the land, out of whole sides they drew the nails and spikes, and with those they made their best instruments. [21]

[19] *The context used here suggests that Amadas and Barlowe's account was written after their return to England. The two natives they refer to as being brought home were Manteo and Wanchese.*

[20] *A reference to the two natives, Manteo and Wanchese, who returned to England.*

[21] *The name of this ship and its origins are unknown.*

Their manner of making their boats is this: they burn down some great tree, or take such as are wind-fallen, and putting myrrh, and rosin upon one side thereof, they set fire into it, and, when it has burned it hollow, they cut out the coal with their shells, and everywhere they would burn it deeper or wider, they lay on their gums, which burn away the timber, and by this means they fashion very fine boats, and such as will transport twenty men. Their oars are like scoops, and many times they set with long poles, as the depth loweth.

The kings brother had great liking of our armour, a sword and diverse other things, which we had: and offered to lay a great bore of pearls in gauge [22] for them: but we refused it for this time, because we would not make them know, that we esteemed thereof, until we had understood in what places of the country the pearl grew: which now your worship does very well understand.

He was very just of his promise: for many times we delivered him merchandise upon his word, but ever he came within the day, and performed his promise. He sent us every day a brace or two of fat Bucks, Conies, hares, fish, the best of the world, he sent us diverse kinds of fruits, melons, walnuts, cucumbers, gourds, peas, and diverse roots, and fruits very excellent good, and of their country corn, which is very white, fair, and well tasted, and grows three times in five months: in May they sow, in July they reap: in June they sow, in August they reap: in July

[22] 'Great bore of pearls in gauge' ~ bore is an old measurement for a barrel; the pearls being termed 'in gauge' meant that they were at least of a diameter considered to give them a marketable value. In essence, a valuable offer by the king's brother!

they sow, in September they reap: only they cast the corn into the ground, breaking a little of the soft turf with a wooden mattock, or pick-axe: ourselves proved the soil, and put some of our peas into the ground, and in ten days they were of fourteen inches high: they have also beans very fair, of diverse colours, and wonderful plenty: some growing naturally, and some in their gardens, and so have they both wheat and oats.

The soil is the most plentiful, sweet, fruitful, and wholesome of all the world: there are about fourteen overall sweet smelling timber trees, and the most part of their underwoods [23] are Bays, and such like: they have those oaks that we have, but far greater, and better.

After they had been diverse times aboard our ships, myself, with seven more, went twenty mile into the river, that runs towards the City of Skicoake, which river they call Occam, [23a] and the evening following, we came to an island, which they call Roanoak, distant from the harbour by which we entered, seven leagues, [24] and at the north end thereof, was a village of nine houses built of cedar, and fortified roundabout with sharp trees, to keep out their enemies, and the entrance into it made like a turnpike very artificially: when we came towards it, standing near unto the waters side, the wife of Granganimeo the King's brother,

[23] 'Underwoods' ~ low-growing shrubs in a wood/ understorey.
[23a] 'Occam' is regarded as being the Pamlico Sound.
[24] The distance from Roanoke to Amadas and Barlowe's ships is therefore about twenty-one to twenty-four miles, or 'seven leagues'. In relation to [6] this would have to equate to the area of Oregon Inlet or Bodie Island because Ocracoke (or 'Wokokon') is at least a direct sixty miles distant from Roanoke; this serves as confirmation in effect that Hakluyt's correction was probably mistaken.

came running out to meet us very cheerfully and friendly, her husband was not then in the village: [25] some of her people she commanded to draw our boat on the shore, for the beating of the billoe: [26] others she appointed to carry us on their backs to the dry ground, and others to bring our oars into the house for fear of stealing.

When we were come into the other room, having five rooms in her house, she caused us to sit down by a great fire, and after took off our clothes, and washed them, and dried them again: some of the women pulled off our stockings, and washed them, some washed our feet in warm water, and she herself took great pains to see all things ordered to the best manner she could, making great haste to dress some meat for us to eat.

After we had thus dried ourselves, she brought us into the inner room, where she sat on the board standing along the house, some wheat like ferment, sodden venison, and roasted, fish sodden, boiled, and roasted, melons raw, and sodden, roots of diverse kinds, and diverse fruits; their drink is commonly water, but while the grapes last, they drink wine [27] and for want of casks to keep it all the year after, they drink water, but it is sodden with ginger in it, and black cinnamon, and sometimes sassafras, and diverse other wholesome, and medicinal herbs and trees.

[25] The Indian village on Roanoke was therefore clearly by the water's edge, close enough to observe passing ships.

[26] 'Billoe' ~ swell (as of the sea).

[27] This is an English assumption. The heat of high summer would cause the grapes (possibly what are known today as Scuppernong, a particularly sweet grape with a high sugar content) to take on a winey taste within a day of being crushed for their juice, due to nothing more than their rapid fermentation.

We were entertained with all love, and kindness, and with as much bounty, after their manner, as they could possibly devise.

We found the people most gentle, loving, and faithful, void of all guile, and treason, and such as lived after the manner of the golden age. The Earth brings forth all things in abundance, as in the first creation, without toil or labour.

The people only care to defend themselves from the cold, in their short winter, and to feed themselves with such meat as the soil affords: their meat is very well sodden, and they make broth very sweet, and savoury: their vessels are earthen pots, very large, white, and sweet: [28] their dishes are wooden platters of sweet timber: within the place where they feed, was their lodging, and within that their idol, which they worship, of which they speak incredible things.

While we were at meat, there came in at the gates, two or three men with their bows and arrows, from hunting, whom when we espied, we began to look one towards another, and offered to reach our weapons: but as soon as she espied our mistrust, she was very much moved, and caused some of her men to run out, and take away their bows, and arrows, and break them, and withal beat the poor fellows out of the gate again.

When we departed in the evening, and would not tarry all night, she was very sorry, and gave us into our boat our supper half dressed, pots, and all, and brought us to our

[28] *'Earthen pots, very large, white, and sweet'* ~ *this does not make sense; large and white pots were used, but sweet is perhaps a typo in the manuscript?*

43

boat's side, in which we lay all night, removing the same a pretty distance from the shore: she perceiving our jealousy, was much grieved, and sent diverse men, and thirty women, to sit all night on the banks side by us, and sent us into our boats fine mats to cover us from the rain, using very many words to entreat us to rest in their houses: but because we were few men, and if we had miscarried, the voyage had been in very great danger, we durst not adventure anything, although there was no cause of doubt: for a more kind, and loving people, there cannot be found in the world, and far as we have hitherto had trial.

Beyond this island, there is the main land, and over against this island falls into this spacious water, the great river called Occam, by the inhabitants, on which stands a town called Pemeoke, [29] and five days journey further up on the same is situated their greatest city called Schycoake, which this people affirm to be very great: but the savages were never at it, only they speak of it, by the report of their fathers, and other men, whom they have heard affirm it, to be above one days journey about. [30]

Into this river falls another great river called Cipo, in which there is found great store of the mussels, in which there are pearls: likewise there descends into this Occam, another river, called Nomopana, [31] on the one side whereof stands a great town, called Chowanoake, and the Lord of that town and country is called Pooneno: this

[29] *'Pemeoke' ~ later referred to as 'Pomeiooc'.*
[30] *Meaning it would take a whole day to walk around it, or see it all.*
[31] *'Nomopana' ~ today known as the Chowan River.*

Pooneno is not subject to the King of Wingandancoa, but is a free Lord. Beyond this country, there is another king, whom they call Menatoan, and these three Kings are in league with each other.

Towards the sunset, some days journey, is situated a town called Sequotan, which is the westernmost town of Wingandacoa, near unto which, five and twenty years past, there was a ship cast away, whereof some of the people were saved, and those were white people, whom the country people preserved. And after ten days, remaining in an out island unhabited, called Wococan, they with the help of some of the dwellers of Sequotan, fastened two boats of the country together, and made mats unto them, and sails of their shirts, and having taken into them such victuals as the country yielded, they departed after they had remained in this out island three weeks: but shortly after, it seemed they were cast away, for the boats were found upon the coast, cast aland in another island adjoining. [32] Other than these, there was never any people apparelled, or white of colour, either seen, or heard of amongst these people, and these aforesaid were seen only of the Inhabitants of Sequotan: which appeared to be very true, for they wondered marvellously when we were amongst them, at the whiteness of our skins, ever coveting to touch our breasts, and to view the same: besides they had our ships in marvellous admiration, and all things else

[32] If these mariners are presumed to have been Spanish, as is most likely, then their intended destination would have been Spanish Florida, possibly Port Royal. The island they were 'cast away' (died) on was obviously south of Wococan (Ocracoke). This could have been what is Portsmouth Island today.

was so strange unto them, as it appeared that none of them had ever seen the like.

When we discharged any piece, were it but a harquebush, they would tremble thereat for very fear, and for the strangeness of the same: for the weapons which themselves use, are bows and arrows: the arrows are but of small canes, headed with a sharp shell, or tooth of a fish [33] sufficient enough to kill a naked man.

Their swords are of wood hardened: likewise they use wooden breastplates for their defence. They have besides a kind of club, in the end whereof they fasten the sharp horns of a stag, or other beast.

When they go to wars, they carry with them their idol, of whom they ask counsel, as the Romans were want of the Oracle of Apollo. They sing songs as they march towards the battle, instead of drums, and trumpets: their wars are very cruel, and bloody, by reason whereof, and of their civil dissentions, which have happened of late years amongst them, the people are marvellously wasted, [34] and in some places, the country left desolate.

Adjoining unto this Town aforesaid, called Sequotan, begins a country called Ponouike, belonging to another King, whom they call Piemacum, and this King is in league with the next King, adjoining towards the setting of the Sun, and the Country Neiosioke, situated upon the side of a goodly river, called Neus: these Kings have mortal war with Wingina, King of Wingandacoa, but about two years

[33] 'Tooth of a fish' ~ possibly a shark or suchlike?
[34] 'Marvellously wasted' ~ an interesting description of something that probably equated to genocide!

past, there was a peace made between the King Piemacum, and the Lord of Sequotan, as these men which we have brought with us into England, have made us understand: but there remains a mortal malice in the Sequotans, for many injuries and slaughters done upon them by this Piemacum.

They invited diverse men, and thirty women, of the best of his Country, to their Town to a feast: and when they were altogether merry, and praying before their Idol, which is nothing else, but a mere illusion of the Devil: the captain or Lord of the Town came suddenly upon them, and slew them every one, reserving the women, and children: and these two have often times since persuaded us to surprise Piemacum his Town, having promised, and assured us, that there will be found in it great store of commodities. But whether there persuasion be to the end they may be revenged of their enemies, or for the love they bear to us, we leave that to the trial hereafter. [35]

Beyond this Island called Croonoake, are many Islands, very plentiful of fruits, and other natural increases, together with many Towns, and villages, along the side of the continent, some bounding along the Islands, and some stretching up further into the land.

When we first had sight of this Country, some thought the first land we saw, to be the continent: but after we entered into the haven, we saw before us another mighty long sea: for there lies along the coast a tract of Islands,

[35] The plot and counterplot relating to the Indian Wars and the temporary but simmering peace agreed upon by the Indians around 1582 is told by Scott Dawson, an authority in the study of the Croatoan tribe, in his book 'Croatoan, Birthplace of America' – See Reference 4.

two hundred miles in length, adjoining to the Ocean Sea, and between the Islands, two or three entrances. [36] When you are entered between them (these Islands being very narrow, for the most part, as in most places five miles broad, in some places less, in few more,) then there appears another great Sea, containing in breadth in some places, forty, and in some fifty, in some twenty miles over, before you come unto the continent: and in this enclosed Sea, there are about a hundred Islands, of diverse bignesses, whereof one is fifteen miles long, at which we were, finding it to be a most pleasant, and fertile ground, replenished with goodly Cedars, and diverse other sweet woods, full of currants, of flax, and many other notable commodities, which we at that time had no leisure to view [37]. Besides this Island, there are many, as I have said, some of two, of three, of four, of five miles, some more, some less, most beautiful, and pleasant to behold, replenished with Deer, Conies, Hares, and diverse beasts, and about them the goodliest and best fish in the world, and in greatest abundance.

Thus Sir, we have acquainted you with the particulars of our discovery, made this present voyage, as far fourth as the shortness of the time we there continued, would afford us to take view of: and so contenting ourselves with this service at this time, which we hope hereafter to enlarge, as occasion and assistance shall be given, we resolved to leave the Country, and apply ourselves to return for England,

[36] *See discussion in Chapter Fourteen.*
[37] *The description here confirms that Amadas and Barlowe were entertained at Roanoke by Granganimeo's wife and this is where they where recommending settlement of the military colony.*

which we did accordingly, and arrived safely in the West of England about the middle of September.

And whereas we have above certified you of the Country, taken in possession by us, to her Majesty's use, and so to yours, by her Majesty's grant, we thought good for the better assurance thereof to record some of the particular Gentlemen, and men of accompaniment, who then were present, as witnesses of the same, that thereby all occasion of cavil to the title of the Country, in her Majesty's behalf, may be presented, which otherwise, such as like not the action may use, and pretend, [38] whose names are:

Master Philip Amadas   Captains
Master Arthur Barlowe

William Grenville [39]   Of the company
John Wood
James Browewich
Henrie Greene
Benjamin Wood
Simon Ferdinando
Nicholas Petman
John Hewes
[40]

[38] *Perhaps to be interpreted as a rather awkward way of saying that any gentleman not among this list but claiming to have seen the land is a liar?*
[39] *This Grenville was almost certainly the brother of George Grenville, a close relative of Sir Richard Grenville. He also served with Drake on his West Indian voyage that relieved Lane's colony in 1586.*
[40] *The 1600 edition closes with the following additional statement:*
'We brought home also two of the Savages being lusty men, whose names were Wanchese and Manteo.'

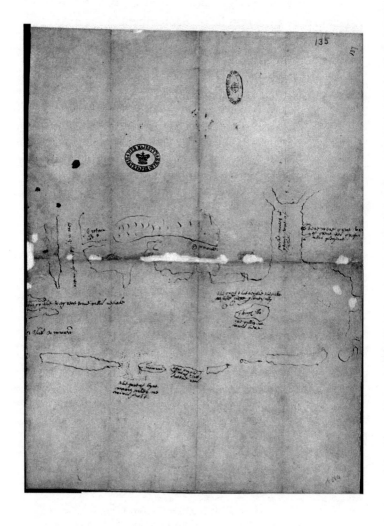

Map reputedly drawn by Captain Arthur Barlowe

Chapter Three

~

The Voyage of Grenville 1585

In 1585 Sir Richard Grenville set out on the first of his voyages to Roanoke. This is the transcription of that voyage.

The Voyage made by Sir Richard Greenvile [1] for Sir Walter Ralegh [2] to Virginia, in the year, 1585.

The 19th day of May, [3] in the year above said, we departed from Plymouth, our fleet consisting of the number of seven sails, to wit, the Tyger, of the burden of seven score tunnes: a fly-boat called the Roe Bucke, of the like burden: the Lyon of a hundred tunnes, or thereabouts: the Elizabeth, of fifty tunnes, and the Dorothie, a small bark, whereunto were also adjoined for speedy services, two small pinnesses.

The principal Gentlemen of our company were, Master Ralfe Lane, Master Thomas Candishe, [4] Master John

[1] 'Greenvile' ~ Grenville; one of many spellings of Sir Richard Grenville's surname.
[2] 'Ralegh' ~ the more common spelling of Raleigh.
[3] This has to be a typographical error else the ships arrived in the Canaries on April 14th, thirty-three days before they left Plymouth; it should read March.
[4] 'Candishe' ~ Cavendish

Arundell, Master Raimund, Master Stukeley, Master Bremige, Master Vincent, and Master John Clarke, and diverse others, whereof some where Captains, and other some Assistants for Counsel, and good directions in the Voyage.

The 14th day of April, we fell with Lancacota, [5] and Forte Ventura, [6] Isle of the Canaries, and from thence we continued our course for Dominica, one of the Antilles of the West India, wherewith we fell the 7th day of May, and the 10th day following, [6a] we came to an anchor at Cotesa, a little Island situate near to the Island of St John, [7] where we landed, and refreshed ourselves all that day.

The 12th day of May, we came to an anchor, in the Bay of Muskito, in the Island of St John, [8] within a Falcon shot [9] of the shore: where our General Sir Richard Greenvill, and the most part of our company landed, and began to fortify, very near to the sea side: the river ran by the one side of our fort, and the other two sides were environed with woods.

The 13th day we began to build a new pinnesse within the fort, with the timber that we then felled in the country, some part whereof we fet [10] three miles up in the land, and brought it to our fort upon trucks, the Spaniards not daring to make or offer resistance.

[5] 'Lancacota' ~ Lanzarote.
[6] 'Forte Ventura' ~ Fuerteventura.
[6a] '10th day following' ~ meaning May 10th.
[7] The island lies just off Puerto Rico.
[8] Grenville spent some time more or less circumnavigating the island of Puerto Rico, for what purpose is unknown.
[9] A falcon or more likely 'falconet' was a small cannon around four feet in length with about a two-inch bore, the best of which had an effective distance of up to a mile.
[10] 'Fet' ~ possible typographical error; likely 'fetched'.

The 16th day, there appeared unto us out of the woods 8 horsemen of the Spaniards, about a quarter of a mile from our fort, staying about half an hour in viewing our forces: but as soon as they saw 10 of our shot marching towards them, they presently retired into the woods.

The 19th day, Master Cavendish, who had been separated from our fleet in a storm in the Bay of Portingal [11] arrived at Cotesa, within the sight of the Tyger: we thinking him a far off to have been either a Spaniard or French Man of War thought it good to weigh anchors, and to go room with him, which the Tyger did, and discerned him at last to be one of our Consorts, for joy of whole coming, our ships discharged their ordinance, and saluted him, according to the manner of the Seas.

The 22nd day, 20 other Spanish horsemen showed themselves to us upon the other side of the river: who being seen, our General dispatched 20 footmen towards them, and two horsemen of ours, mounted upon Spanish horses, which we before had taken in the time of our being on the Island: they showed to our men a flag of truce, and made signs to have a parley with us: whereupon two of our men went half of the way upon the sands, and two of theirs came and met them: the two Spaniards offered very great Salutations to our men, but began according to their Spanish proud humours, to expostulate with them, about their arrival and fortifying in their country, who not withstanding by our men's discrete answers were so cooled, that they were told, that our principal intention was only to furnish ourselves with water, and victuals, and

[11] 'Portingal' ~ Portugal.

other necessaries whereof we stood in need, which we craved might be yielded us with faire, and friendly means, otherwise our resolution was to practice force, and to relieve ourselves by the sword: the Spaniards in conclusion, seeing our men so resolute, yielded to our requests with large promises of all courtesy, and great favour, and so our men and theirs departed. [11a]

The 23rd day our pinnesse was finished, and launched, which being done, our General with his Captains, and Gentlemen, marched up into the country about the space of 4 miles where in a plain marsh, they stayed expecting the coming of the Spaniards according to their promise, to furnish us with victuals: who keeping their old custom for perjury and breach of promise came not, whereupon our General fired the woods thereabouts, and so retired to our fort, which the same day was fired also, and each man came aboard to be ready to set sail the next morning.

The 24th day we set sail from St Johns, being many of us stung before upon shore with the mosquitoes: but the same night, we took a Spanish frigate, which was forsaken by the Spaniards upon the sight of us, and the next day in the morning very early, we took another frigate, with good

---

[11a] *We can gain the Spanish version of this incident from the records acquired by Martin Fernandez de Navarette, a Spanish naval commander and historian (1765-1844), in which there is a letter from Diego Hernandez do Quinones, the governor at Havana, Cuba, to King Philip of Spain. It records that the governor of Puerto Rico sent thirty-five arquebusiers (mounted riflemen) and forty soldiers to view what Grenville was up to at the fort. The Spanish version declares that the English stated that they had Spanish prisoners and intended to sell them in Florida, the suggestion being that they would be put to the sword if the Spanish did not let the English finish building their boat. (Translation from* Further English Voyages to Spanish America 1583-1594, *edited by Irene A. Wright, Hakluyt Society 1951.)*

and rich freight, and diverse Spaniards of accompaniment in her, which afterwards we ransomed for good round sums, and landed them in Saint Johns. [14a]

The 26th day our Lieutenant Master Ralfe Lane, went in one of the frigates which we had taken, to Roxo bay [12] upon the Southwest side of Saint Johns, to fetch salt, being thither conducted by a Spanish pilot: as soon as he arrived there, he landed with his men, to the number of 20, and entrenched himself upon the sands immediately, compassing one of their salt hills within the trench: who being seen of the Spaniards, there came down towards him two or three troops of horsemen, and footmen, who gave him the looking, and gazing on, but durst not come near him to offer any resistance, so that Master Lane mauger [12a] their troops, carried their salt aboard and loaded his frigate, and so returned again to our fleet the 29th day, which rode at Saint Germans Bay. The same day we all departed, and the next day arrived in the Island of Hispaniola.

June

The first day of June we anchored at Isabella, in the North side of Hispaniola

The 3rd day of June, the Governor of Isabella, and Captain of the Port de Plata, being certified by the reports of sundry Spaniards, who had been well entertained aboard

[12] *Now known as Cabo Rojo, Puerto Rico. See also John White's drawing of Lane's fort.*
[12a] *'Mauger' ~ meaning 'in spite of'.*

our ships by our General, that in our fleet were many brave, and gallant Gentlemen, who greatly desired to see the Governor aforesaid, he thereupon sent gentle commendations to our General, promising within few days to come to come to him in person, which he performed accordingly.

The 5th day the foresaid governor, accompanied with a lusty friar, and other Spaniards, with their servants and Negroes, came down to the sea side, where our ships rode at anchor, who being seen, our General manned immediately the most part of his boats with chief men of our fleet, every man appointed, and furnished in the best sort: at the landing of our General, the Spanish Governor received him very courteously, and the Spanish Gentlemen saluted our English Gentlemen, and their inferior sort did also salute our Soldiers and Seamen, liking our men, and likewise their qualities, although at the first, they seemed to stand in fear of us, and of so many of our boats, whereof they desired that all might not land their men, yet in the end, the courtesies that passed on both sides were so great, that all fear and mistrust on the Spaniards part was abandoned.

In the meantime while our English General and the Spanish Governor discoursed betwixt them of diverse matters, as of the state of the Country, the multitude of the Towns and people, and the Commodities of the island, our men provided two banqueting houses covered with green boughs, the one for the Gentlemen, the other for the servants, and a sumptuous banquet was brought in served by us all in Plate, with the sound of trumpets, and consort of music wherewith the Spaniards were more than delighted.

Which banquet being ended, the Spaniards in recompense of our courtesy, caused a great herd of white bulls, and kine, [13] to be brought together from the Mountains, and appointed for every Gentlemen and captain that would ride, a horse ready saddled, and then singled out three of the best of them to be hunted by horsemen after their manner, so that the pastime grew very pleasant, for the space of three hours, wherein all three of the beasts were killed, whereof one took the sea, and there was slain with a musket.

After this sport, many rare presents and gifts were given and bestowed on both parts, and the next day we placed the Merchants in bargaining with them by way of truck and exchange for diverse of their commodities, as horses, [14] mares, kine, bulls, goats, swine, sheep, bull hides, sugar, ginger, pearl, tobacco, and such like commodities of the Island. [14a]

The 7th day we departed with great good will from the Spaniards from the Island of Hispaniola: but the wiser

[13] 'Kine' ~ old English word for cow.

[14] This is clear evidence the Grenville's vessel did have Spanish horses on board when it arrived at the Outer Banks. Might the progeny of these bartered-for horses of Hispaniola be the Ocracoke Banker horses of today (See discussion Chapter Fourteen)?

[14a] The same letter referenced at [11a] also reveals that at the time of writing (to King Philip of Spain) the English had five ships moored at Hispaniola and were 'demanding' horses and cattle and victuals. Interestingly the governor also recorded that they had two Indians on board 'richly dressed'.

The letter then goes on to include the account of Don Fernando de Altamirano, captain of the Spanish frigate captured by the English on May 24th. Altamirano states that the English had told him they were exploring the West Indies with a view to asking Spain to consider joint rule, their authority for being there supposedly granted to them by 'a great English lord' (Raleigh) and their admiral being one 'Richarte de Campo Verde' (Grenville). Altamirano finishes by noting that the two Indians on board spoke 'good English and were great lovers of music'.

sort do impute this great show of friendship, and courtesy used towards us by the Spaniards rather to the force that we were of, and the vigilance, and watchfulness that was amongst us, than to any hearty good will, or sure friendly entertainment: for doubtless if they had been stronger than we, we might have looked for no better courtesy at their hands, than Master John Hawkins received at Saint John de Ulua, [15] or John Oxnam near the straits of Dariene, [16] and diverse others of our Countrymen in other places.

The 8th day we anchored at a small Island to take seals which in that place we understood to have been in great quantity, where the General and certain others with him in the Pinnesse, were in very great danger to have been cast away, but by the help of God they escaped the hazard, and returned aboard the Admiral in safety.

The 9th day we arrived and landed in the Isles of Caicos, in which Island we searched for salt ponds, upon the advertisement and information of a Portingall: who indeed abused our General and us, deserving a halter for his hire, [17] if it had so pleased us.

The 12th day we anchored at Guanema, [18] and landed. The 15th and 16th, we anchored and landed at Sygateo [18]

[15] 'Saint John de Ulua' ~ more correctly San Juan de Ullua, a fort by the port of Veracruz, Mexico. In 1568, Sir John Hawkins (in company with Sir Francis Drake) was set upon by a sizeable Spanish fleet and barely escaped in the ensuing battle.

[16] 'John Oxnam… straits of Dariene' ~ John Oxenham was an English privateer who crossed the Isthmus of Panama to plunder Spanish shipping in the Pacific Ocean. He was finally captured and taken to Panama City, and later Lima, Peru, where he was executed for piracy in 1580.

[17] 'Halter for his hire' ~ effectively a 'noose around his neck'.

[18] Localities unidentified. From the course given, these were or are locations in the northern Turks and Caicos or the Bahamas.

The 20th we fell with the main of Florida. The 23rd we were in great danger of a wreck on a breech called the Cape of Feare. The 24th we came to anchor in a harbour where we caught in one tide so much fish as would have yielded us 20 pounds in London: this was our first landing in Florida. The 26th we came to anchor at Wocokon. The 29th we weighed anchor to bring the Tyger into the harbour, where through the unskillfulness of the Master whose name was Fernando, the Admiral stroke on ground, and sunk. [18a]

July

The 3rd we sent word of our arriving at Wococon, to Wingino at Roanoke.

The 6th Master John Arundell was sent to the main, and Manteo with him: and Captain Aubry, and Captain Boniten the same day were sent to Croatoan, where they found two of our men left there, with 30 other by Captain Reymond, some 20 days before. [18b]

The 8th Captain Aubry, and Captain Boniten returned with two of our men found by them to us at Wococon.

The 11th day the General accompanied in his Tilt boat with Master John Arundell, Master Stukelye, and diverse other Gentlemen, Master Lane, Master Candish, Master Harriot, and 20 others in the new pinnesse, Captain Amadas,

[18a] *Not sunk but badly damaged and later repaired.*
[18b] *Captain Reymond was in charge of the Red Lyon. The narrative does not record their separation from the fleet but it is reasonable to assume this took place during the storm off Portugal.*

Captain Clarke, with ten others in a ship boat, Francis Brooke, and John White in another ship boat passed over the water from Ococon to the mainland victualled for eight days, in which voyage we first discovered the Towns at Pomioke, Aquascogoc, and Secota, and also the great lake called by the savages Paquype, [19] with diverse other places, and so returned with that discovery to our fleet.

The 12th we came to the Town of Pomeioke. The 13th we passed by water to Aquascococke. The 15th we came to Secotan and were well entertained there of the savages. The 16th we returned thence, and one of our boats with the Admiral was sent to Aquascococke to demand a silver cup which one of the savages had stolen from us, and not receiving it according to his promise, we burnt, and spoiled their corn, and Town, all the people being fled. [20]

The 18th we returned from the discovery of Secotan, and the same day came aboard our fleet riding at Wocokon. The 21st our fleet anchoring at Wokocon, we weighed anchor for Hatoraske. The 27th our fleet anchored at Hatoraske, and there we rested. The 29th, Grangino, brother to King Wingino, came aboard the Admiral, and Manteo with him. [21]

August

The 2nd The Admiral was sent to Weapemeoke. The 5th Master John Arundell was sent for England. The 25th our

[19] 'Paquype' ~ Lake Mattamuskeet?
[20] The word 'fled' is interpreted and transcribed as 'sled' or 'slayed' in other editions but in this edition the word is clearly spelled 'fledde'.
[21] Grenville met King Wingina and Manteo on board his flagship Tyger.

General weighed anchor, and set sail for England. About the 31st he took a Spanish ship of 300 tunne richly laden, boarding her with a boat made with boards of chests, [22] which fell asunder, and sunk at the ships side, as soon as ever he and his men were out of it.

September

The 10th of September, by foul weather the General then shipped in the prize lost sight of the Tyger.

October

The 1st the Tyger fell with the Land's End, [23] and the same day came to anchor at Falmouth [24]. The 18th, the General came with the prize to Plymouth, and was courteously received by diverse of his worshipful friends.

* * *

On August 12th Ralph Lane wrote three letters from Roanoke,

[22] *Grenville is recorded as having taken this ship (the Santa Maria de Vincenze) with thirty of his men by rowing across to it on a makeshift raft of sea chests, which promptly sunk as they boarded the ship. Again, we are fortunate to have an eyewitness account from a Portuguese merchant (Enrique Lopez) on board the captured ship. In his report he remarks that Grenville was a great man, his food served on silver plates and accompanied by the playing of music [Coleccion Navarette XXV 53]. The ship was sailed back to Bideford (with Grenville on board) where it was converted to become the Dudley.*
[23] *'Land's End' ~ the most south-westerly point of the English mainland.*
[24] *'Falmouth' ~ Principal deepwater port on the south coast of Cornwall approximately midway between Land's End and Plymouth.*

which were recorded in the Calendar of State Papers Colonial Series *as follows:*

Aug. 12 1585
Port Ferdinando Virginia. Ralph Lane to Sec. Walsingham.

The Generals return to England cuts him off from reporting upon the peculiarities of the country. Although they arrived there late in the year, wholly through the fault of him who intends to accuse others, they have nevertheless discovered so many rare and singular commodities in the Queen's new kingdom of Virginia, as by the universal opinion of all the apothecaries and merchants there, no state in Christendom doth yield better or more plentiful. Leaves the particulars to the General's report; the ship's freight will prevent all suspicion of fraud. They have not yet found one stinking weed growing in the land.

Describes the vast and huge territory, its natural fortifications, and the climate very healthy: There are only three entries and ports; these they have named, Trinity, Scarborough, and Ococan, [25] where their fleet struck aground, and the Tyger was nearly lost: The best port discovered by Simon Ferdinando, the master and pilot major of the fleet, after whom it is named, and which, if fortified by a sconce, could not be entered by the whole force of Spain. Account of their soundings. Has undertaken with a good company to remain there, resolute rather to lose their lives "than to defer possession" of so noble a kingdom to the Queen, their country, and their

[25] *See discussion in Chapter Fourteen.*

noble patron Sir Walter Raleigh, through whose and his Honour's most worthy endeavour and infinite charge an honourable entry is made to the conquest of. Is assured they will, by this means, be relieved from the tyranny of Spain, and their enemies, the Papists, will not be suffered by God to triumph at the overthrow either of this most Christian action, or of His poor servants, in their thorough famine or other wants. God will command even the ravens to feed them.

* * *

Aug. 12 1585
Port Ferdinando Virginia. Ralph Lane to Walsingham.

Commends to his favour the bearer, Mr. Atkinson, who carried himself so honestly and industriously throughout the voyage. Has also written by Mr. Russell to the like effect, and is persuaded, notwithstanding the general displeasure towards Atkinson that he will clear himself of every charge or imputation.

* * *

Aug. 12 1585
Port Ferdinando Virginia. Lane to Sir Philip Sydney.

Will not omit writing to him, although in the midst of infinite business, having the charge of savages as well as wild men of his own nation, whose unruliness prevents his leaving them. Refers him to his letter to Mr. Secretary for an account of the singularities of Virginia. Has discovered the infinite riches of St. John and Hispaniola by dwelling upon the islands five weeks. Thinks if the Queen should find herself burdened with the King of Spain, that to attempt them would be most honourable, feasible, and profitable. Exhorts him not to refuse the good opportunity of rendering so great a service to the Church of Christ, he only being fit for the chief command of such an expedition. The strength of Spain doth altogether grow from the mines of her treasure.

On September 8th Ralph Lane wrote a letter from Port Ferdinando, which was recorded in the Calendar of State Papers Colonial Series *as follows:*

Sept. 8 1585
From the New Fort in Virginia. Lane to Sec. Walsingham.

Has thought good to advertise him concerning Sir R. Greenefeelde's [26] complaints against sundry gentlemen of this service, and particularly against Mr. Candyshe their high marshal, Edward. George, Francis Brooke, their treasurer, and Capt. Clerck. Certifies to their faithfulness and industry, and to the tyrannical conduct of Grenville from first to last, through whose great default the action has been made most painful and most perilous. Refers him to an ample discourse of the whole voyage in the hands of the bearer, their treasurer, directed to Sir W. Raleigh, wherein Grenville's intolerable pride, insatiable ambition,

---

[26] *'Greenefeelde' ~ yet another spelling of Grenville.*

and proceedings towards them all, and to Lane in particular, are set forth. Has had so much experience of Grenville as to desire to be freed from the place where he is to carry any authority in chief. They have discovered a kind of Gynneye [27] wheat, that yields both corn and sugar, of which their physician bath sent an assay to Sir W. Raleigh. There are fertile and pleasant provinces in the main land, populated only by savages, fit to be civilly and christianly inhabited. Means, with the favour of God, to visit them and pass some part of the winter in their provinces, 140 miles within the main.

* * *

Hakluyt's transcripts then continue with a listing of the military colonists under Ralph Lane's charge.

The names of all those as well Gentlemen as others that remained one whole year in Virginia, under the Government of Master Ralfe Lane.

Master Philip Amades, Admiral of the country	Master Thomas Harvie
	Master Snelling
Master Hariot	Master Anthony Russe
Master Acton	Master Allyne
Master Edward Stafford	Master Michel Polyson
Thomas Luddington	John Cage
Master Marvyn	Thomas Parre
Master Gardiner	William Randes

[27] 'Gynneye' ~ Guinea wheat or Indian corn.

Captain Vaughan
Master Kendall
Master Prideox
Robert Holecroft
Rise Courtney
Master Hugh Rogers
Thomas Foxe
Edward Nugen
Darby Glande
Edward Kelle
John Gostigo
Erasinus Clefs [30]
Edward Ketcheman
John Linsey
Thomas Rottenbury
Roger Deane
John Harris
Frauncis Norris
Matthewe Lyne
Edward Kettell
Thomas Wisse
Robert Biscombe
William Backhouse
William White
Henry Potkin
Dennis Barnes
Joseph Borges
Doughan Gannes [30]

Geffery Churchman
William Farthowe
John Taylor
Phillipe Robyns
Thomas Phillippes
Valentine Beale
James Skinner
George Eseven
John Chaundeler
Philip Blunt
Richard Poore
Robert Yong
Marmaduke Constable
Thomas Hesket
William Wasse
John Fever
Daniel [28]
Thomas Taylor
Richard Humfrey
John Wright
Gabriell North
Bennet Chappell
Richard Sare
James Lacie
Smolkin
Thomas Smart
Robert [28]
John Evans

[28] Given the meticulous recording of names, these are probably cabin boys, who were often waifs and strays or orphans and thus probably never had a known surname.

William Tenche
Randall Latham
Thomas Hulme
Walter Myll
Richard Gilbert
Steven Pomarie
John Brocke
Bennet Harrye
James Stevenson
Charles Stevenson
Christopher Lowde
Jeremy Man
James Mason
David Salter
Richard Ireland
Thomas Bookener
William Phillppes
Randall Mayne

Roger Large
Humfrey Garden
Frauncis Whitton
Rowland Griffyn
William Millard
John Twyt
Edward Seklemore
John Anwike
Christopher Marshall
David Williams
Nicholas Swabber
Edward Chipping
Sylvester Beching
Vincent Cheyne
Haunce Walters [29]
Edward Barecombe
Thomas Skevelabs [30]
William Walters

[29] This can only be 'Haunce the surgeon' recorded as drowning in a boat capsized during an attempted landing in the voyage of 1590.
[30] These could be Bohemians, who at the time were known for their alchemy. Since one of the objectives of the voyage was to establish the relative wealth that might be gained from minerals in the New World, this theory is not unrealistic.

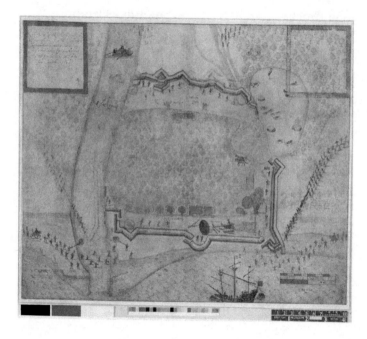

Ralph Lane's Fort at Tallaboa Bay

Chapter Four

~

The Military Colony of 1585 (Part One)

Ralph Lane recorded his stay on the Outer Banks in two parts. The first part is transcribed below.

An account of the particularities of the employments of the English men left in Virginia by Sir Richard Greenevill under the charge of Master Ralfe Lane General of the same, from the 17 of August 1585 until the 18 of June 1586, at which time they departed the country: sent, and directed to Sir Walter Ralegh.

That I may proceed with order in this discourse, I think it requite to divide into two parts. The first shall declare the particularities of such parts of the Country within the main, as our weak number, and supply of things necessary did enable us to enter into the discovery thereof. The second part, shall set down the reasons generally moving us to resolve on our departure at the instant with the general Sir Francis Drake, and our common request for passage with him, when the barks, pinnesses, and boats with the Masters and Mariners meant by him to be left in the Country for the supply of such, as for a further time meant to have stayed there were carried away with tempest, and foul weather: In the beginning whereof shall be declared the conspiracy of Pemisapan, [1] with the Savages of the main to have cut us off.

The first part declaring the particularities of the countrey of Virginia.

First therefore touching the particularities of the Country, you shall understand our discovery of the same hath been extended from the Island of Roanoak, (the same having been the place of our settlement or inhabitation) into the South, into the North, into the Northwest, and into the West. The uttermost place to the Southward of any discovery was Secotan, being by estimation four score miles distant from Roanoak. [2]

The passage from thence was through a broad sound within the main, the same being without kenning of land, [3] and yet full of flats and shoals: we had but our boat with four oars to pass through the same, which boat could not carry above fifteen men with their furniture, [4] baggage, and victual for seven days at the most: and as for our Pinnesse, besides that she drew too deep water for that shallow sound, she would not stir for an oar: for these

[1] 'Pemisapan' ~ Scott Dawson, an authority on the early native Indians of the Outer Banks region, states that all Indian names had meaning; however, the name Pemisapan has no known meaning in the Croatoan language.
[2] Ralph Lane's calculation places Secotan near to present-day Belhaven on the Pungo River.
[3] 'Kenning of land' ~ to say 'not knowing or recognising any land' i.e. no islands in this interpretation. The Broad Sound referred to is the Pamlico Sound today.
[4] 'Furniture' ~ meaning their weapons.

and other reasons (winter also being at hand) we though good wholly to leave the discovery of those parts until our stronger supply. [5]

To the Northward our furthest discovery was to the Chesepians, distant from Roanoak about 130 miles, the passage to it was very shallow and most dangerous, by reason of the breadth of the sound, and the little succour that upon any shore was there to be had. [6]

But the territory and the soil of the Chesepians (being distant fifteen miles from the shore) was for pleasantness of seat, for Temperature of Climate, for fertility of soil, and for the commodity of the Sea, besides multitude of bears (being an excellent good victual, with great woods of Sassafras and Walnut trees) is not to be excelled by any other whatsoever. [7]

There be sundry Kings, whom they call Weroances, and Countries of great fertility adjoining to the same, as the Mandoages, Tripanicks, and Opossians, which all came to visit the Colony of the English, which I had for a time appointed to be resident there. [8]

To the Northwest the farthest place of our discovery was to Choanoke distant from Roanoak about 130 miles. Our passage thither lay through a broad sound, but all free

[5] *This makes it clear that Lane was not interested in visiting Secotan or the Pamlico Sound in any detail until his hoped-for fresh supplies arrived in the spring.*

[6] *Given Lane's geographic accuracies in his compass directions, this description can only refer to the Currituck Sound. The distance recorded of 130 miles is extraordinary as this would take Lane up around the entrance to the Chesapeake Bay and as far as the James River.*

[7] *This statement provides a persuasive argument by which to influence Raleigh in the preferred location of the 1587 colony.*

[8] *This makes it clear that somewhere on the James River there may be another English fort that predates the discovery of the original Jamestown fort.*

water, and the channel of great depth, navigable for good shipping, but out of the channel full of shoals. [9]

The towns about the waterside situated by the way, are these following: Pysshokonnok, The womans Towne, Chipanum, Weopomiok, Muscamunge, and Mattaquen: all these being under the Jurisdiciton of the King of Weopemiok, called Okisco: from Muscamunge we enter into the River, and jurisdiction of Choanoke: There the River begins to straighten until it come to Choanoke, and then grows to be as narrow as the Thames between Westminster and Lambeth. [10]

Between Muscamunge and Choanoke upon the left hand as we pass thither, is a goodly high land, and there is a Town which we called the blind Town, but the Savages called it Ooanoke, and has a very goodly cornfield belonging unto it: it is a subject to Choanoke.

Choanoke itself is the greatest Province and Seigniory lying upon that River, and the very Town itself is able to put 700, fighting men into the field, besides the forces of the Province itself.

The King of the said Province is called Menatonon, a man impotent in his limbs, but otherwise for a Savage, a very grave and wise man, and of very singular good discourse in matters concerning the state, not only of his own Country, and the disposition of his own men, but also of his neighbours around about him as well far as near, and of the commodities that each Country yielded.

[9] The site of Choanoke is widely regarded as being Edenton, but if Lane's calculations are correct then Edenton is some fifty miles short of the site visited by the military colonists. The nearest settlement would be Winton, less than twenty miles from the Virginia border.
[10] About eight hundred feet.

When I had him prisoner with me, for two days that we were together, he gave me more understanding and light of the Country than I had received by all the searches and savages that before I or any of my company had had conference with: it was in March last past 1586.

Amongst other things he told me, that going three days journey in a canoe by his River of Choanoke, and then descending to the land, you are within four days journey to pass over land Northeast to a certain Kings country, whose Province lies upon the sea, but his place of greatest strength is an Island situate as he described unto me in a Bay, the water round about the Island very deep. [11]

Out of this Bay he signified to me, that this King had so great a quantity of Pearl, and does so ordinarily take the same, as that not only his own skins that he wears, and the better sort of his gentlemen and followers, are full set with the said Pearl, but also his beds, and houses are garnished with them, and that he has such quantity of them, that it is a wonder to see.

He showed me that the said King was with him at Choanoak two years before, and brought him certain Pearl, but the same of the worst sort, yet was he feign to buy them off him for copper at a dear rate as he thought: He gave me a rope of the same Pearl, but they were black and naught, yet many of them were very great, and a few amongst a number very orient and round, all which I lost with other things of mine, coming aboard Sir Francis

[11] *Difficult to determine where this island could be. It is not inconceivable that the 'island' could be misinterpreted as the southern tip of Cape Charles, Maryland.*

Drake his fleet: yet he told me that the said King had great store of Pearl that were white, great, and round, and that his black Pearl his men did take out of shallow water, but the white Pearl his men sifted for in very deep water.

It seemed to me by his speech, that the said King had trafficked with white men that had clothes as we have [12] for these white Pearl, and that was the reason that he would not depart with other than black Pearls, to those of the same Country.

The King of Choanoak promised to give me guides to go overland into that Kings Country whensoever I would: but he advised me to take good store of men with me, and good store of victual, for he said, that King would be loath to suffer any strangers to enter into his Country, and especially to meddle with the fishing for any Pearl there, and that he was able to make a great many of men into the field, which he said would fight very well.

Whereupon I resolved with myself, that if your supply had come before the end of April, and that you had sent any store of boats, or men, to have them made in any reasonable time, with a sufficient number of men, and victuals to have found us until the new corn were come in, I would have sent a small Bark with two Pinesses about by Sea to the Northward to have found out the Bay he spoke of, and to have sounded the bar if there were any, which should have ridden there in the said Bay about the Island, while I with all the small Boats I could make, and with two

[12] *This suggests either specific contact with Englishmen or it could be more generic in nature. There are, however, no known accounts of such contact with native Indians in the Chesapeake Bay area in the years leading up to this account.*

hundred men would have gone up to the head of the River of Choanoak, with the guides that Menatonon would have given, which I would have been assured should have been of his best men, (for I had his best beloved son prisoner with me) who also should have kept me company in an handlock with the rest foot by foot all the voyage over land.

My meaning was further at the head of the River in the place of my descent where I would have left my boats to have raised a sconce [13] with a small trench, and a palisade upon the top of it, in the which, and in the guard of my Boats I would have left five and twenty, or thirty men, with the rest would I have marched with as much victual as every man could have carried, with their furniture, mattocks, spades, and ares, two days journey.

In the end of the march upon some convenient plot would I have raised another sconce according to the former, where I would have left 15 or 20. And if it would have fallen out conveniently, in the way I would have raised my said sconce upon some cornfield that my company might have lived upon it.

And so I would have holden this course of ensconcing every two days march, until I had been arrived at the Bay or Port he spoke of: which finding to be worth the possession, I would there have raised a main fort, both for the defence of the harboroughs, and our shipping also, and would have reduced our whole habitation from Roanoak and from harborough and port there (which by proof is very naught) unto this other before mentioned,

[13] 'Sconce' ~ military fort.

from whence, in the four days march before specified could I at all times return with my company back unto my boats riding under my sconce, very near whereunto directly from the West run a most notable River, and in all those parts most famous, called the River of Morotico. [14]

This River opens into the broad sound of Weopomiok: And whereas the River of Choanoak, and all the other sounds, and Bays, salt and fresh, show no current in the world in calm weather, but are moved altogether with the wind: This River of Morotico has so violent a current from the West and Southwest, that it made me almost of opinion that with oars it would scarce be navigable: it passes with many creeks and turnings, and for the space of thirty miles rowing and more, it is as broad as the Thames betwixt Greenwich, and the Isle of Dogs, [15] in some places more, and in some less: the current runs as strong being entered so high into the River, [16] as at London Bridge upon a bale water.

And for that not only Menatonon, but also the Savages of Morotico themselves do report strange things of the head of that River, and that from Morotico itself, which is a principal Town upon that River, it is thirty days as some of them say, and some say forty days voyage to the head thereof, which head they say springs out of a main rock in that abundance, that forthwith it makes a most violent stream: and further, that this huge rock stands near unto a Sea, that many times in storms (the wind coming outwardly

[14] *The Morotico River could be the James River, a location that Lane was clearly intending to relocate the colony to and which John Smith headed for in 1607.*
[15] *About a thousand feet.*
[16] *'Entered so high into the River' ~ as in a waterfall?*

from the Sea) the waves there are beaten into the said fresh stream, so that the fresh water for a certain space, grows salt and brackish: [17]

I took a resolution with myself, having dismissed Menatonon upon a ransom agreed for, and sent his son into the Pinnesse to Roanoak, to enter presently so far into that River with two double wherries, and forty persons one or other, as I could have victual to carry us, until we could meet with more either of the Moratiks, or of the Mangoaks which is another kind of Savages, dwelling more to the Westward of the said River: but the hope of recovering more victual from the Savages made me and my company as narrowly to escape starving in that discourse before our return, as ever men did that missed the same.

For Pemisapan, who had changed his name of Wingina upon the death of his brother Granganimeo, had given both the Choanists and Mangoaks word of my purpose touching them, I having been enforced to make him privy to the same, to be served by him of a guide to the Mangoaks, and yet he did never rest to solicit continually my going upon them, certifying me of a general assembly even at that time made by Menatonon at Choanoak of all his Weroances, and allies to the number of 3,000 bows preparing to come upon us at Roanoak and that the Mangoaks also were joined in the same confederacy, who were able of themselves to bring as many more to the enterprise:

[17] *Is Menatonon simply retelling a myth? The location he describes has yet to be formally identified.*

And true it was, that at this time the assembly was held at Choanoak about us, as I found at my coming thither, which being unlooked for did so dismay them, as it made us have the better hand at them. But this confederacy against us of the Choanists and Mangoaks was altogether and wholly procured by Pemisapan himself, as Menatonon confessed unto me, who sent them continual word that our purpose was fully bent to destroy them: on the other side he told me that they had the like meaning towards us.

He in like sort having sent word to the Mangoaks of mine intention to pass up into their River, and to kill them (as he said) both they and the Moratiks, with whom before we were entered into a league, and they had ever dealt kindly with us, abandoned their Towns along the River, and retired themselves with their Crenepoes, [18] and their corn within the main:

Insomuch as having passed three days voyage up the River, we could not meet a man, nor find a grain of corn in their Towns: whereupon considering with myself, that we had but two days victual left, and that we were then 160 miles [19] from home, besides casualty of contrary winds or storms, and suspecting treason of our own Savages in the discovery of our voyage intended, though we had no intention to be hurtful to any of them, otherwise for our copper to have had corn of them:

[18] 'Crenepoes' ~ the font used for this word in the original text is the distinct form used for all native Indian tribal names and races of people, but they are not mentioned elsewhere in the text. The answer is in the 1600 version where there is a margin note stating 'Their women'.
[19] This estimate would have taken them approximately forty miles over the state border with modern Virginia.

I at night upon the Corps of Guard, before the putting forth of sentinels, advertised the whole company of the case we stood in for victuals, and of mine opinion that we were betrayed by our own Savages, and of purpose drawn forth by them, upon vain hope to be in the end starved, seeing all the fled before us, and therefore while we had those two days victual left, I thought it good for us to make our return homeward, and that it were necessary for us to get the other side of the sound of Weopomiok in time, where we might be relieved upon the weirs of Chypanum, and the womans Town, although the people were fled.

Thus much I signified unto them, as the safest way: nevertheless, I did refer it to the greatest number of voices, whether we should adventure the spending of our whole victual in some further view of that most goodly River in hope to meet some better hap, or otherwise to retire ourselves back again: And for that they might be the better advised, I willed them to deliberate all night upon the matter, and in the morning at our going aboard to set our course according to the desires of the greatest part. Their resolution fully and wholly was (and not three found to be of the contrary opinion) that while there was left one half pint of corn for a man, that we should not leave the search of that River, and that there were in the company two mastiffs, upon the pottage of which with sassafras leaves (if the worst fell out) the company would makeshift to live two days, which time would bring them down the current to the mouth of the River, and to the entry of the sound, and in two days more at the farthest they hoped to cross the sound and to be relieved by the weirs, which two days they would fall rather than be drawn back a foot till they had seen the Mangoaks, either as friends or foes.

This resolution of theirs did not a little please me, since it came of themselves, although for mistrust of that which afterwards did happen, I pretended to have been rather of the contrary opinion.

And that which made me most desirous to have some doings with the Mangoaks either in friendship or otherwise to have had one or two of them prisoners, was, for yet is it a thing most notorious to all ye country, that there is a Province to the which said Mangoaks have recourse and traffic up that River of Morattico, which has a marvellous and most strange Mineral. This mine is so notorious amongst them, as not only to the Savages dwelling up by the said river, and also to the Savages of Choanoke, and all them to the westward, but also to all them of the main: the countries name is of same, and is called Chaunis Temoatan.

The mineral they say is Wassador, which is copper, but they call by the name of Wassador every metal whatsoever: they say it is of the colour of our copper, but our copper is better than theirs: and the reason for that it is redder and harder, whereas that of Chaunis Temoatan is very soft, and pale: they say that they take the said metal out of a river that falls very swift from high rocks, and hills, and they take it in shallow water: the manner is this.

They take a great bowl by their description as great as one of our targets, and wrap a skin over the hollow part thereof, leaving one part open to receive in the mineral: that done, they watch the coming down of the current, and the change of the colour of the water, and then suddenly chop down the said bowl with the skin, and receive into the same as much ore as will come in, which is ever as much as their bowl will hold, which presently they cast into a fire, and forthwith it melts, and does yield in five parts, at the first melting, two parts of metal for three parts of ore. [20]

Of this metal the Mangoaks have so great a store, by report of all the Savages adjoining, that they beautify their houses with great plates of the same: and this to be true, I received by report of all the country, and particularly by young Skiko, the King of Choanokes son of my prisoner, who also himself had been prisoner with the Mangoaks, and set down all the particularities to me before mentioned: but he has not been at Chawnis Temoatan himself: for he said, it was twenty days journey overland from the mangoaks, to the said mineral country, and that they passed through certain other territories between them and the Mangoaks, before they came to the said country.

Upon report of the premises, which I was very inquisitive in all places where I came to take very particular information of, by all the savages that dwell towards those parts, and especially of Menatonon himself, who in everything did very particularly inform me, and promised me guides of his own men, who should pass over with me, even to the said country of Chaunis Temoatan, (for over land from Choanoak to the Mangoaks is but one days journey from sun rising to sun setting, whereas by water it is 7 days with the soonest:)

These things I say, made me very desirous by all means

[20] *The true identification of the metal described here is discussed in Chapter 14.*

possible to recover the Mangoaks, and to get some of their copper for an assay, and therefore I willingly yielded to their resolution: But it fell out very contrary to all expectation, and likelihood: for after two days travel, and our whole victual spent, lying on shore all night, we could never see man, only fires we might perceive made along the shore where we were to pass, and up into the country until the very last day. In the evening whereof, about three of the clock we heard certain Savages call as we thought, Manteo, who was also at that time with me in boat, whereof we all being very glad, hoping of some friendly conference with them, and making him to answer them: they presently began a song, as we thought in token of our welcome to them: but Manteo presently betook him to his piece, and told me that they meant to fight with us: which word was not so soon spoken by him, and the light horsemen ready to put to shore, but there lighted a volley of their arrows amongst them in the boat, but did no hurt God be thanked to any man.

Immediately, the other boat lying ready with their shot to secure the place for our hand weapons to land upon, which was presently done, although the land was very high and steep, the Savages forthwith quitted the shore, and betook themselves to flight: we landed, and having fair and easily followed for a small time after them, who had wooded themselves we know not where: the sun then drawing towards the setting, and being then assured that the next day, if we would pursue them, though we might happen to meet with them, yet we should be assured to meet with none of their victual, which we then had good cause to think of, therefore choosing for the company convenient ground in safety to lodge in for the night, making a strong Corps of Guard, and putting out good sentinels.

I determined the next morning before the rising of the sun to be going back again, if possibly we might recover the mouth of the river into the broad sound, which at my first motion I found my whole company ready to assent unto: for they were now come to their dogs porridge, that they had bespoken for themselves, it that befell them which did, and I before did mistrust we should barely escape.

The end was, we came the next day by night to the rivers mouth within 4 or 5 miles of the same: having rowed in one day down the current, as much as in 4 days we had done against the same: we lodged upon an Island, where we had nothing in the world to eat but pottage of sassafras leaves, the like whereof for a meat was never used before as I think.

The broad sound we had to pass, the next day all fresh and salting: that day the wind blew so strongly, and the billow so great, that there was no possibility of passage without sinking our boats. This was upon Easter eve, [21] which was fallen very truly.

Upon Easter day in the morning the wind coming very calm, we entered the sound, and by 4 of the clock we were at Chipanum, where all the Savages that we had left there were fled, but their weirs did yield us some fish, as God was pleased not utterly to suffer us to be lost for some of our company of the light horsemen were far spent.

[21] 'Easter eve' ~ the Saturday before Easter Sunday. In 1586 this 'Easter eve' would have been April 2nd.

The next morning we arrived at our home Roanoke.

I have set down this voyage somewhat particularly, to the end it may appear unto you, (as true it is) that there wanted no great goodwill from the most to the least amongst us, to have perfited [22] this discourse of the mine: for that discovery of a good mine, by the goodness of God, or a passage to the South Sea, or someway to it, and nothing else can bring this country in request to be inhabited by our nation.

And with the discovery of any of the two above shown, it will be the most sweet, and beautiful climate, and there withal the most fertile soil, being manured for the world: and then will Sassafras, and many other roots and gums there found make good Merchandise and lading for shipping, which otherwise of themselves will not be worth the fetching.

Provided also, that there be found out a better Harborough then yet there is, which must be to the Northward, if any there be, which was mine intention to have spent this summer in the search of, and of the mine of Chawnis Temoatan: the one I would have done, if the barks that I should have had of Sir Francis Drake, by his honourable coutesy, had not been driven away by storm: the other if your supply of more men, and some other necessaries had come to us in any convenient sufficiency. For this river of Moratico promised great things, and by the opinion of Master Harriots the head of it by the description of the country, either rises from the bay of

[22] 'Perfited' ~ meaning 'perfected'.

Mexico, or else from very near unto the same, that opens out into the South Sea. [23]

And touching the Mineral, thus does Master Yougham affirm that though it be but copper, seeing the Savages are able to melt it, it is one of the richest Minerals in the world.

Wherefore a good Harborough found to the Northward, as before is said, and from thence four days overland, to the river of Choanoak sconces being raised, from whence again overland through the province of Choanoak one days voyage to the first town of the Mangoaks up the river of Moratico by the way, as also upon the said river for the defence of our boats like sconces being set, in this course of proceedings you shall clear yourself from all those dangers and broad shallow sounds before mentioned, and grain within four days travel into the heart of the main 200 miles at the least, and to pass your discovery into that most notable, and to the likeliest parts of the main, with far greater felicity than otherwise can be performed.

Thus sir, I have though simply, yet truly set down unto you, what my labour with the rest of the gentlemen, and poor men of our company, (not without both pain, and peril which the Lord in his mercy many ways delivered us

[23] The Indians describe falls in the river. Given that Lane and Harriot would have known their general direction in navigating the river, they clearly knew they were heading westerly or south-westerly. From the Indian description and the text from Lane, it is likely the river being navigated was the Nottoway. A possible location for the falls would be those about thirty miles south of Petersburg, Virginia, in which case, if Lane's mileage calculations were accurate, then they were very close to these falls when they turned back. Since this is the location of the metal described by the Indians, this may also explain why the Indians attacked, fearing the discovery of their source of wealth.

from) could yield unto you, which might have been performed in some more perfection, if the lord had been pleased that only that which you had provided for us had at the first been left with us, or that he had not in his eternal providence now at the last set some other course in these things, then the wisdom of man could look into, which truly the carrying away, by a most strange, and unlooked for storm all our provision, with barks, master, mariners, and sundry also of mine own company, all having been so courteously supplied by the General Sir Francis Drake, the same having been most sufficient to have performed the greatest part of the premises, must ever make me think, the hand of God only, for some his good purpose to myself yet unknown, to have been in the matter. [24]

[24] *For all Lane's efforts, this paragraph appears to be an apology to Raleigh!*

Ralph Lane's fort at Caba Rojo

Chapter Five

~

The Military Colony of 1585 (Part Two)

The second part of Ralph Lane's account of the military colony's occupation.

The Second Part touching the conspiracy of Pemisapan, the discoverie of the same, and at the last, of our request to depart with S. Francis Drake for England.

Ensenore a savage father to Pemisapan being the only friend to our nation that we had amongst them, and about the King, died the 20th April 1586, he alone, had before opposed himself in their consultations against all matters proposed against us, which both the King, and all the rest of them after Granganimeo's death, were very willing to have preferred. And he was not only by the mere providence of God during his life, a thieve to save us from hurt, as poisonings and such like, but also to do us very great good, and singularly in this.

The King was advised and of himself disposed, as a ready mean to have assuredly brought us to ruin in the month of March 1586 himself also with all his Savages to have run away from us, and to have left his ground in the Island unsowed, which if he had done, there had been no possibility in common reason, (but by the immediate hand of God) that we could have been preserved from starving out of hand. For at that time we had no weirs for fish, neither could our men skill of the making of them, neither had we one grain of corn for seed to put into the ground.

In mine absence on my voyage that I had against the Chaonists, and Mangoaks, they had raised a bruite [1] among themselves, that I and my company were part slain, and part starved by the Chaonists, and Mangoaks. One part of this tale was too true: that I and mine were like to be starved, but the other false.

Nevertheless until my return, it took such effect in Pemisapans breast, and those against us, that they grew not only into contempt of us, but also (contrary to their former reverend opinion in show, of the almighty God of heaven, and Jesus Christ, whom we serve and worship, whom before they would acknowledge and confess the only God:) now they began to blaspheme, and flatly to say, that our Lord God was not God, since he suffered us to sustain much hunger, and also to be killed of the Renapoaks, for so they call by that general name, all the inhabitants of the whole main, of what province soever. Insomuch as old Ensenore, neither any of his fellows, could for his sake have no more credit for us: and it came so far that the King was resolved to have presently gone away as is aforesaid.

But even in the beginning of this bruite I returned,

[1] 'Bruite' ~ a rumour

which when he saw contrary to his expectation, and the advertisement that he had received: that not only myself, and my company were all safe, but also by report of his own 3 Savages, which had been with me besides Manteo in that voyage, that is to say, Tetepano, his sisters husband Eracano, and Cossine, that the Choanists, and Mangoaks, (whose name, and multitude besides their valour is terrible to all the rest of the provinces) durst not for the most part of them abide us, and that those that did abide us were killed, and that we had taken Menatonon prisoner, and brought his son that he best loved to Roanoak with me, it did not a little assuage all devices against us: on the other side, it made Ensenore's opinions to be received again with greater respects.

For he had often before told them, and then renewed those his former speeches, both to the King and the rest, that we were the servants of God, and that we were not subject to be destroyed by them: but contrarywise, that they amongst them that fought our destruction, should find their own, and not be able to work ours, and that we being dead men were able to do them more hurt, then now we could do being alive: an opinion very confidently at this day holden by the wisest amongst them, and of their old men, as also, that they have been in the night, being 100 miles from any of us in the air shot at, and stroken by some men of ours, that by sickness had died among them: and many of them hold opinion, that we be dead men returned into the world again, and that we do not remain dead but for a certain time, and that then we return again.

All these speeches then again grew in full credit with

them, the King and all touching us, when he saw the small troup returned again, and in that sort from those whose names were terrible unto them: but that which made up the matter on our side for that time, was an accident, yea rather, (as all the rest was) the good providence of the Almighty for the saving of us, which this was.

Within certain days after my return from the said journey, Menatonon sent a messenger to visit his son the prisoner with me, and sent me certain pearl for a present, or rather as Pemisapan told me, for the ransom of his son, and therefore I refused them: but the greatest cause of his sending them, was to signal unto me, that he had commanded Okisko King of Weopomiok, to yield himself servant, and homager, to the great Weroanza of England, and after her to Sir Walter Raleigh: to perform which commandment received from Menatonon, the said Okisko jointly with this Menatonon messenger, sent four and twenty of his principal men to Roanoak to Pemisapan, to signal that they were ready to perform the same, and so had sent those his men to let me know, that from that time forward he, and his successors were to acknowledge her Majesty their only Sovereign, and next unto her, as is aforesaid.

All which being done, and acknowledged by them all, in the presence of Pemisapan his father, and all his Savages in counsel then with him, it did for the time, thorough (as it seemed) change him in disposition towards us: Insomuch as forthwith Ensenore was this resolution of him, that out of hand he should go about and withal, to cause his men to set up weirs forthwith for us: both which he, at that present went in hand withal and did so labour the expedition of it, that in the end of April, he had sowed a good quantity of ground, so much as had been sufficient, to have fed our whole company (God blessing the growth) and that by the belly for a whole year: besides that he gave us a certain plot of ground for ourselves to sow.

All which put us in marvellous comfort, if we could pass from April, until the beginning of July, (which was to have been the beginning of their harvest,) that then a new supply out of England or else our own store would well enough maintain us:

All our fear was of the two months betwixt, in which mean space, if the Savages should not help us with Cassada, [2] and Chyna, and that our weirs should fail us, (as often as they did,) we might very well starve, notwithstanding the growing corn, like the starving horse in stable, with the growing grass as the proverb is, which we very hardly had escaped but only by the hand of God, as it pleased him to try us.

For within few days after, as before is said Ensenore our friend died, who was no sooner dead, but certain our great enemies about Pemisapan, as Osocan a Weroance, Tanaquiny and Wanchese most principally, were in hand again to put their old practices in use against us, which we readily embraced, and all their former devices against us renewed, and new brought in question.

But that of starving us, by their forbearing to sow, was broken by Ensenore in his life, by having made the King all at one instant to sow his ground not only in the Island but also at Addesinocopeia in the main, within two leagues

[2] 'Cassada' ~ cassava.

over against us. Nevertheless there wanted no store of mischievous practices among them, and of all they resolved principally of this following.

First that Okisko, king of Weopomiok, with the Mandoages, should be moved, and with great quantity of copper entertained to the number of seven or 800 bows to the enterprise the matter thus to be ordered.

They of Weopomiok should be invited to a certain kind of months mind [3] which they do use to solemnise in their Savage manner for any great personage dead, and should have been for Ensenore.

At this instant also should the Mangoaks who were a great people with the Chesepians, and their friends to the number 700, of them to be armed at a day appointed to the main of Addesmocopeio, and there lying close at the sign of fires, which should interchangeably be made on both sides, when Pemisapan with his troup above named should have executed me, and some of our Weroances (as they called all our principal officers,) the main force of the rest should have come over into the Island where they meant to have despatched the rest of the company, whom they did imagine to find both dismayed and dispersed abroad in the Island seeking of crabs, and fish to live withall.

The manner of their enterprise was this.

Tarraquine and Andacon two principal men about Pemisapan, and very lusty fellows with twenty more appointed to them had the charge of my person to see an

[3] *'Months mind' ~ an ancient service or feast held in honour of a dead person, one month after their death.*

order taken for the same, which they meant should in this sort have been executed.

In the dead time of the night they would have beset my house, and put fire in the reeds, that the same was covered with: meaning (as it was likely) that myself would have come running out a sudden amazed in my shirt without arms, upon the instant whereof they would have knocked out my brains.

The same order was given to certain of his fellows, for Master Harriots: so for all the rest of our better sort, all our houses at one instant being set on fire as afore is said, and that as well for them of the fort, as for us at the town. [4]

Now to the end that we might be the fewer in number together, and so be the more easily dealt withal (for indeed ten of us with our arms prepared, were a terror to a hundred of the best sort of them,) they agreed and did immediately put it in practice, that they should not for any copper, sell us any victuals whatsoever: besides that in the night they should send to have our weirs robbed, and also to cause them to be broken and once being broken never to be repaired again by them.

By this means the King stood assured, that I must be enforced for lack of sustenance, there to disband my company into sundry places to live upon shellfish, for so the Savages themselves do, going to Ottorasko, [5] Crotoan, and other places fishing and hunting, while their

[4] *Confirmation of the existence of a fort and that Lane and his officers probably had separate lodgings, possibly living with or by the native Indians at their village on Roanoke (almost certainly the same village where Granganimeo's wife had shown them hospitality).*
[5] *'Ottorasko' ~ Hatorask?*

grounds be in sowing, and their corn growing, which failed not his expectation.

For the famine grew to extreme among us, our weirs failing us of fish, that I was enforced to send Captain Stafford with 20 with him to Crotoan my lord Admirals Island [5a] to serve two turns in one, that is to say to feed himself and his company, and also to keep watch, if any shipping came upon the coast to warn us of the same, I sent Master Prideox with the Pinnesse to Otterasco, and ten with him, with the Provost Marshall to live there, and also to wait for shipping: also I sent every week 16 or so of the rest of the company to the main over against us, to live off Cassava, and others. [6]

In the meanwhile Pemisapan went as purpose to Addesinocopeio for 3 causes, the one to see his grounds there broken up, and sowed for a second crop: the other to withdraw himself from my daily sending to him for supply of victual for my company, for he was afraid to deny me anything, neither durst he in my presence but by colour, and with excuses, which I was content to accept for the time, meaning in the end as I had reason, to give him the jump once for all: but in the meanwhile, as I had ever done before, I and mine bare all wrongs, and accepted of all excuses.

My purpose was to have relied myself with Menatonon, and the Chaonists, who in truth as they are more valiant people and in greater number then the rest, so are they

[5a] *A confused comment since 'Lord Admiral' refers to Grenville and Grenville's 'Island' was Wocokon (Ocracoke,) the island his flagship (the Tyger) foundered on, not Hatteras ('Crotoan'). Grenville did not land on Hatteras so far as records indicate.*
[6] *With twenty on Croatoan (Hatteras) and ten on Hatorask (?), sending sixteen men every week to the mainland would have evacuated Roanoke in about five weeks.*

more faithful in their promises, and since my late being there, had given many tokens of earnest desire they had to join in perfect league with us, and therefore were greatly offended with Pemisapan and Weopomiok for making him believe such tales of us.

The third cause of his going to Addesmacopeio was to despatch his messengers to Weopomiok, and to the Mandoages, as aforesaid, all which he did with great impress of copper in hand, making large promises to them of greater spoil.

The answer within few days after, came from Weopomiok, which was divided into two parts, first for King Okisko, who denied to be of any party for himself, or any of his especial followers, and therefore did immediately retire himself with his force into the main: the other was concerning the rest of the said province who accepted of it: and in like sort the Mandoags received the imprest. [7]

The day of their assembly aforesaid at Roanoke, was appointed the 10 of July: all which the premises were discovered by Skyco, the King Menatonon his son my prisoner, who having once attempted to run away, I laid him in the bilboes, [8] threatening to cut off his head, whom I remitted at Pemisapans request: whereupon he being persuaded that he was our enemy to the death, he did not only feed him with himself, but also made him acquainted with all his practices.

On the other side, the young man finding himself as

[7] 'Imprest' ~ in this context, something received from a government for services rendered.
[8] 'Bilboes' ~ iron shackles.

well used at my hand, as I had means to show, and that all my company made much of him, he flatly discovered all unto me, which also afterwards was revealed unto me by one of Pemisapans own men, by night before he was slain.

These mischief's being all instantly upon me, and my company to be put in execution, stood me in hand to study how to prevent them, and also to save all others, which were at that time as aforesaid to fair from me: whereupon I sent to Pemisapan to put suspicion out of his head, that I meant presently to go to Crotoan, for that I had heard of the arrival of our fleet, (though I in truth had neither heard nor hoped for so good adventure,) and that I meant to come by him, to borrow of his men to fish for my country, and to hunt for me at Crotoan, as also to buy some four days provision to serve for my voyage.

He sent me word that he would himself come over to Roanoak, but from day to day he deferred, only to bring the Weopomioks with him, and the Mandoags, whose time appointed was within 8 days after.

It was the last of May 1586, when all his own Savages began to make their assembly at Roanoak, at his commandment sent abroad unto them, and I resolved not to stay longer upon his coming over, since he meant to come with so good company, but thought good to go, and visit him with such as I had, which I resolved to do the next day: but that night I meant by the way to give them in the Island a Canuisado, and at the instant to seize upon all the Canoas about the Island to keep him from advertisements.

But the town took the alarm, before I meant it to them. The occasion was this:

I had sent the Master of the light horsemen with a few with him, to gather up all the Canoas in the setting of the sun, and to take as many as were going from us to Adesmocopeio, but to suffer any that came from thence to land: he met with a Canoa, going from the shore, and overthrew the Canoa, and cut off 2 Savages heads: this was not done so secretly but he was discovered from the shore, whereupon the cry arose: for in truth they, privy to their own villainous purposes against us, held as good espial upon us, both day and night, as we did upon them. The alarm given, they took themselves to their bows, and we to our arms: some three or four of them at the first were slain with our shot, the rest fled into the woods:

The next morning with the light horseman, and one Canoa, taking 25, with the Colonel of the Chesepians, and the Sergeant Major, I went to Adesmocopeio, and being landed sent Pemisapan word by one of his own Savages that met me at the shore, that I was going to Crotoan, and meant to take him in the way to complain unto him of Osocon, who the night past was conveying away my prisoner, whom I had there present tied in a Handlock: hereupon the King did abide my coming to him and finding myself amidst 7 or 8 of his principal Weroances, and followers (not regarding any of the common sort) I gave the watchword agreed upon, (which was Christ our victory,) and immediately those his chief men, and himself, had by the mercy of God for our deliverance, that which they had purposed for us.

The King himself being shot thorough by the Colonel with a pistol lying on the ground for dead, and I looking as watchfully for the saving of Manteo's friends, as others were busy that none of the rest should escape, suddenly he started by and ran away as though he had not been touched, insomuch as he overran all the company, being by the way shot through the buttocks by mine Fresh boy with my Petronell. [9]

In the end a Fresh-man serving me, one Nugent and the deputy provost [10] undertook him, and following him in the woods overtook him, and I in some doubt least we had lost both the King, and my man by our own negligence to have been intercepted by the Savages, we met him returning out of the woods with Pemisapans head in his hand.

This fell out the first of June 1586, and the 8 of the same came advertisement to me from Captain Stafford, lying at my lord Admiral's Island, that he had discovered a great fleet of 23 sails: but whether they were friends or foes, he could not yet discern, he advised me to stand upon as good guard as I could.

The 9 of the said month, he himself came unto me, having that night before, and that same day travelled by land 20 miles, and I must truly report of him from the first to the last, he was the gentleman that never spared labour or peril either by land or water, for weather or foul, to perform any service committed unto him.

He brought me a letter from the General Sir Francis Drake, with a most bountiful and honourable offer for the supply of our necessities to the performance of the action,

[9] 'Petronell' ~ a large-calibre gun.
[10] 'Nugent and the Deputy Provost' ~ this confirms that the deputy provost of Ralph Lane's company was Edward Nugent ('Nugen' in the list of names given in Hakluyt's list ~ see Chapter Three.) Thus it was Edward Nugent who cut off Pemisapan's head.

we were entered into, and that not only of victuals, munitions and clothing, but also of barks, pinnaces and boats, they also by him to be victualled, manned, and furnished to my contentation. [11]

The 10 day he arrived in the road of our bad Harborough, and coming there to an anchor, the 11 day I came to him, whom I found in deeds most honourably to perform that which in writing and message he had most courteously offered, he having aforehand propounded the matter to all the captains of his fleet, and got their liking and consent thereto.

With such thanks unto him and his captains for his care of us and of our action, not as the matter deserved, but as I could both for my company and myself, I (aforehand) prepared what I would desire, craved at his hands that it would please him to take with him into England a number of weak, and unfit men for my good action, which I would deliver to him, and in place of them to supply me of his company, with oarsmen, artificers, and others.

That he would leave us so much shipping and victual, as about August then next following, would carry me and all my company into England, when we had discovered somewhat that for lack of needful provision in time left with us as yet remained undone. [12]

That it would please him withal to leave some sufficient masters not only to carry us into England when time

[11] 'Contentation' ~ meaning 'satisfaction'.
[12] This awkward paragraph expresses that Lane hoped Drake would leave him enough ships to ensure that if things did not work out for the colony he had enough means by which to return to England with his men that August.

should be, but also to search the coast for some better Harborough if there were any, and especially to help us to some small boats and oarsmen.

Also for a supply of Calievers, [13] handweapons, match and lead, tools, apparel and such like.

He having received these my requests according to his usual commendable manner of government (as it was told me) calling his captains to counsel, the resolution was that I should send such of my officers of my company, as I used in such matters, with their notes to go aboard with him, which were the master of the victuals, the keeper of the store, and the vice treasurer, to whom he appointed forthwith for me the Francis, being a very proper barke of 70 tunnes, [13a] and took present order for bringing of victual aboard her for 100 men for four months withal my other demands whatsoever, to the uttermost.

And further appointed for me two fine pinnaces, and 4 small boats, and that which was to perform all his former liberality towards us, was that he had gotten the full assents of two of as sufficient experimented [14] master as were any in his fleet, by judgement of them that knew them, with very sufficient gings [15] to tarry [16] with me, and to employ themselves most earnestly in the action, as I should

[13] 'Calievers' ~ 'calivers', a smaller version of the arquebus rifle.
[13a] According to Thomas Cate's account aboard the Primrose, the captain of the Francis was Thomas Moone. (From A Summarie and True Discourse of Sir Francis Drakes West Indian Voyage published by Richard Field of Blackfriars in 1589 and reprinted with commentary below.)
[14] 'Experimented' ~ probably intended to be 'experienced' (a typographical error?).
[15] 'Gings' ~ meaning a troop or a crew.
[16] 'Tarry' ~ a word of multiple meanings, popularly meaning 'to delay' but in this context meaning 'stay temporarily'.

appoint them, until the term which I promised of our return into England again. [17] The names of one of those masters was Abraham Kendall, the other Griffith Herne.

While these things were in hand, the provision aforesaid being brought, and in bringing aboard, my said masters being also gone abroad, my said barks having accepted of their charge, and mine own officers with others in like sort of my company with them, all which was dispatched by the said General the 12 of the said month: the 13 of the same there arose such an unwanted storm, and continued four days that had like to have driven all on shore, if the Lord had not held his holy hand over them, and the General very providently foreseen the worst himself, then about my dispatch putting himself aboard: but in the end having driven sundry of the fleet to put to sea, the Francis also with all my provisions, my two masters, and my company aboard, she was seen to be free from the same, and to put clear to sea.

This storm having continued from the 13 to the 16 of the month, and thus my bark put away as aforesaid, the General coming ashore, made a new proffer to me, which was a ship of 170 tunnes, called the Bark Bonner, with a sufficient master and guide to tarry with me the time appointed, and victualled sufficiently to carry me and my company into England with all provisions as before: but he told me that he would not for anything undertake to

[17] *It is clear from this statement and Lane's earlier reference to August that he did not intend to overwinter a second year on Roanoke, meaning that in any event he planned to leave in but three months regardless.*

have her brought into our harbour, and therefore he was to leave her in the road, and to leave the care of the rest unto myself, and advised me to consider with my company of our case, and to deliver presently unto him in writing, what I would require him to do for us: which being within his power, he did assure me as well for his Captains, as for himself should be most willingly performed.

Hereupon calling such Captains and Gentlemen of my company as then were at hand, who were all as privy as myself to the Generals offer, their whole request was to me, that considering the case that we stood in, the weaknesses of our company, the small number of the same, the carrying away of our first appointed barke, with those two especial masters, with our principal provisions in the same, by the very hand of God as it seemed, stretched out to take us from thence: considering also, that his second offer, though most honourable of his part, yet of ours not to be taken, insomuch as there was no possibility for her with any safety to be brought into the harbour:

Seeing furthermore our hope for supply with Sir Richard Greenvill so undoubtedly promised us before Easter, not yet come, neither then likely to come this year considering the doings in England for Flanders, as also for America, that therefore I would resolve myself, with my company to go into England in that fleet, and accordingly to make request to the General in all our names, that he would be pleased to give us present passage with him.

Which request of ours by myself delivered unto him, he most readily assented unto, and so he sending immediately his pinnaces unto our Island for the fetching away of few that there were left with our baggage, the weather was so boisterous, and the pinnaces so often on ground, that the most of all we had, with all our Cards, Books and writings, were by the Sailors cast overboard, the greater number of the fleet being much aggrieved with their long and dangerous abode in that miserable road.

From whence the General in the name of the almighty, weighing his anchor (having bestowed us among his fleet) for the relief of whom he had in that storm sustained more peril of wreck then in all his former most honourable actions against the Spaniards, with praises unto God for all, set sail the 19 June 1586, and arrived in Portsmouth, the 27 of July the same year.

* * *

The Account of Thomas Cate

This brief account is the eyewitness record of a member of Drake's crew regarding the relief of Ralph Lane's colony.

* * *

"The ninth of June upon sight of one special great fire (which are very ordinary all along this coast, even from Cape Florida hither) the General sent his Skiff to the shore, where they found some of our English countrymen (that had been sent thither the year before by Sir Walter Raleigh) and brought one aboard, by whose direction we proceeded along to the place, which they make their Port. But some of our ships being of great draught unable to enter, we anchored all without the harbour in a wild road at sea, about two miles from shore.

From whence the General wrote letters to Master Ralfe Lane, being Governor of those English in Virginia, and then at his fort about six leagues from the road in an Island, which they call Roanoac, wherein specially he showed how ready he was to supply his necessities and wants, which he understood of, by those he had first talked withal.

The morrow after Master Lane himself and some of his company coming unto him, with the consent of his Captains, he gave them the choice of two offers, that is to say: Either he would leave a ship, a Pinnace, and certain boats with sufficient Masters and mariners, together furnished with a months victual to stay and make further discovery of the country and coasts, and so much victual likewise that might be sufficient for the bringing of them all (being an hundred and three persons) [18] into England if they thought good after such time, with any other thing they would desire, and that he might be able to spare.

Or else if they thought they had made sufficient discovery already, and did desire to return into England, he would give them passage. But they as it seemed, being delirious to stay, accepted very thankfully, and with great gladness that which was offered first.

Whereupon the ship being appointed and received into charge, by some of their own company sent into her by

[18] Lane landed with 107 men and left with 103 according to this account, which leaves four men unaccounted for. It is necessary to refer to Pedro Diaz's account (see Chapter Nine) for a record of their probable demise at the hands of the Indians.

Master Lane, before they had received from the rest of the Fleet, the provision appointed them, there arose a great storm (which they said was extraordinary and very strange) that lasted three days together, and put all our Fleet in great danger, to be driven from their anchoring upon the coast.

For we broke many cables, and lost many anchors. And some of our Fleet which had lost all (of which number was the ship appointed for Master Lane and his company) were driven to put to sea in great danger, in avoiding the coast, and could never see us again until we met in England. Many also of our small Pinnaces and boats were lost in this storm.

Notwithstanding after all this, the General offered them (with consent of his Captains) another ship with some provision, although not such a one for their turns, as might have been spared them before, this being unable to be brought into their harbour. Or else if they would, to give them passage into England, although he knew he should perform it with greater difficulty then he might have done before.

But Master Lane with those of the chiefest of his company he had then with him, considering what should be best for them to do, made request unto the General under their hands, that they might have passage for England: the which being granted, and the rest sent for out of the country and shipped, we departed from the coast the eighteenth of June."

Note: The account puts the value of Drake's prizes at £60,000 and the loss of men at 'some seven hundred fifty'.

* * *

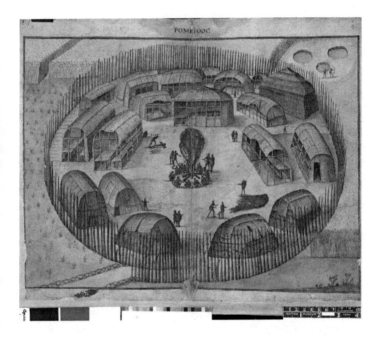

The Village of Pomeiooc

Chapter Six

~

The Voyages of 1586

In 1586 two voyages set sail to supply Ralph Lane's colony, arriving barely days after their relief at the hands of Drake. This is Hakluyt's account of those voyages.

The third voyage made by a Ship, sent in the yeere 1586. To the reliefe of the Colonie planted in Virginia, at the sole charges of Sir Walter Raleigh.

In the year of our Lord, 1586, Sir Walter Raleigh at his own charge prepared a ship of 100 tunnes, freighted with all manner of things in most plentiful manner for the supply and relief of his Colony then remaining in Virginia: but before they set sail from England, it was after Easter, so that our Colony half despaired of the coming of any supply, wherefore every man prepared for himself, determining resolutely to spend the residue of their lifetime in that country, and for the better performance of this their determination, they sowed, planted, and set such things as were necessary for their relief in so plentiful a manner, as might have sufficed them two years without any further labour:

Thus trusting to their own harvest they passed the summer till the tenth of June, at which time their corn which they had sowed was within one fortnight of reaping, but then it happened, that Sir Francis Drake in his prosperous return from the sacking of Saint Domingo, Cartagena, and Saint Augustines determined in his way homeward to visit his countrymen the English Colony then remaining in Virginia: so passing along the coasts of Florida, he fell with the partes, where our English Colony inhabited, and having espied some of that company, there he anchored, and went aland where he conferred with them of their state and welfare, and how things had passed with them: they answered him that they lived all, [1] but hitherto in some scarcity, and as yet could hear of no supply out of England:

Therefore they requested him that he would leave with them some two or three ships, that if in some reasonable time they heard not out of England, they might then return themselves: which he agreed to:

While some were then writing their letters to send into England, and some others making reports of the accidents of their travels each to other, some on land, some on board, a great storm arose, and drove the most of their fleet from their anchors to Sea, in which ships, at that instant were the chiefest of the English Colony:

The rest on land perceiving this, hasted to those three sails which were appointed to be left there, and for fear they should be left behind, left all things so confused, as if

[1] The report by Thomas Cate states there were four men missing at the time of departure; this is further supported by the deposition of Pedro Diaz, who states that the Indians had killed four.

they had been chased from thence by a mighty army, and no doubt they were, for the hand of God came upon them for the cruelty, and outrages committed by some of them against the native inhabitants of that Country. [2]

Immediately after the departing of our English Colony out of this paradise of the world, the ship above mentioned sent, and set forth at the charges of Sir Walter Raleigh, and his direction, arrived at Hatorask, who after some time spent in seeking our Colony up in the Country, and not finding them, returned with all the aforesaid provisions into England.

About fourteen or fifteen days after the departure of the aforesaid ship, Sir Richard Grindfield [3] General of Virginia, accompanied with three ships well appointed for the same voyage arrived there, [4] who not finding the aforesaid ship [5] according to his expectation, nor hearing any news of our English Colony, there seated, and left by him anno 1585, himself travelling up into diverse places of the Country, as well [6] to see if he could hear any news of the Colony [7] left there by him the year before, under

[2] *This is quite a different perception of the events leading to the abandonment of Virginia by Lane's colony. 'For fear they should be left behind' does not suggest an orderly withdrawal from the settlement. However, the final sentences regarding the 'hand of God' and the 'cruelty, and outrages committed' are clearly subjective comments by the author (Hakluyt) and so should not be accepted as a factual account of that abandonment but more as a dramatization for the benefit of readers, perhaps.*

[3] *'Grindfield' ~ another spelling of Grenville.*

[4] *In the margin of the original transcript the words 'Grenville's third voyage' are written. However, only two voyages are known at this point in history: the 1585 voyage of the military colony and this one of 1586.*

[5] *Suggesting that Raleigh's supply ship should have known to wait for Grenville to arrive?*

[6] *Suggesting Grenville explored the Outer Banks region in some detail in search of the colony.*

[7] *'Hear any news' ~ this could well mean that Grenville spoke to the native Indians. We know from Pedro Diaz's deposition of 1589 that he captured three Indians in a skirmish and kept one as prisoner. The latter almost certainly was the 'Rawley' of St Mary's Parish Church, Bideford.*

the charge of Master Lane his deputy, as also to discover some places of the Country:

But after some time spent therein not hearing any news of them, and finding the place which they inhabited desolate, yet unwilling to lose the possession of the Country, which Englishmen had so long held: after good deliberation he determined to leave some men behind to retain possession of the Country: whereupon he landed 15 men in the Isle of Roanoke furnished plentifully with all manner of provision for two years, and so departed for England.

Not long after he fell with the Isles of the Azores, on some of which Islands he landed, and spoiled the Towns of all such things as were worth carriage, where also he took diverse Spaniards: [8] with these, and many other exploits done by him in this voyage, as well outwards as homeward, he returned into England.

[8] 'Took diverse Spaniards' ~ according to Pedro Diaz, Grenville used twenty-two Spaniards as slaves in the building of his house in Bideford. These came from the taking of the Santa Maria de Vincenze and from here in the Azores.

A Weroance (Indian Chief)

Chapter Seven

~

The Planters' Colony of 1587

This, the story of the planters' colony, is what has become known as the Lost Colony.

The fourth voyage made to Virginia, with three shippes, in the yeare 1587. Wherein was transported the Second Colonie.

In the year of our Lord, 1587, Sir Walter Raleigh intending to persevere in the planting of his Country of Virginia, prepared a new Colony of one hundred and fifty men to be sent thither, under the charge of John White, whom he appointed Governor, and also appointed unto him twelve Assistants, unto whom he gave a Charter, and incorporated them by the name of Governor and Assistants of the Cittie of Ralegh in Virginia. [1]

April

Our Fleet being in the number three sail, viz, the Admiral,

[1] Hakluyt here records 150 planters, whilst Pedro Diaz in his deposition reports that Grenville was trying to raise a colony of 210.

a ship of one hundred and twenty tunnes: a flyboat, and a Pinnesse, departed the six and twentieth of April from Portsmouth, and the same day came to an anchor at the Cowes, [1a] in the Isle of Wight, where we stayed eight days.

May

The 5 of May, at nine of the clock at night, we came to Plymouth, where we remained the space of two days.

The 8 we weighed anchor at Plymouth, and departed thence to Virginia.

The 16 Simon Ferdinando Master of our Admiral, lewdly forsook our flyboat, leaving her distressed in the Bay of Portingall.

June

The 19 we fell with Dominica, and the same evening we sailed between it and Guadalupe: the 21 the flyboat also fell with Dominica.

The 22 we came to an anchor at an Isle, called Santa Cruz, where all the planters were set on land, staying there till the 25 of the same month. At our first landing on this Island, some of our women, and men, by eating a small fruit, like green apples, were fearfully troubled with a

[1a] *Cowes is a popular yachting town on the Isle of Wight. The reason for staying at Cowes for eight days is currently unexplained.*

sudden burning in their mouths, and swelling of their tongues so big, that some of them could not speak. Also a child by sucking on one of those women's breast, [2] had at that instant his mouth set on such a burning, that it was strange to see how the infant was tormented for the time: [3] but after 24 hours, it wear away of itself.

Also the first night of our being on this Island, we took five great Tortoises, some of them such bignes, that sixteen of our strongest men were tired with carrying of one of them but from the Sea side, to our cabins. In this Island we found no watering place, but a standing pond, the water whereof was so evil, that many of our company fell sick with drinking thereof: and as many as did but wash their faces with that water, in the morning before the Sun had drawn away the corruption, their faces did so burn, and swell, that their eyes were shut up, and could not see in five or six days, or longer.

The second day of our abode there, we sent forth some of our men to search the Island for fresh water, three one way, and two another way. The Governor also, with six others, went up to the top of an high hill, to view the Island, but could perceive no sign of any men, or beasts, nor any goodness, but Parrots and trees of Guiacum. [4]

Returning back to our cabins another way, he found in

[2] *There were only two women on the voyage with children named as their own: Joyce Archard and her son Thomas and Elizabeth Viccars and her son Ambrose.*

[3] *Two fruits could be attributed to this description but since one of them is deadly, it is likely the colonists tried to eat unripe black sapote fruit, which would yield these symptoms.*

[4] *'Guiacum' ~ lignum vitae; probably known to the English via the Spanish as a source of treatment for syphilis, a condition widespread in Europe at the time.*

the descent of a hill, certain potsherds Savage making, made of the earth of that Island: whereupon it was judged, that this Island was inhabited with Savages, though Fernando had told us for certain to the contrary.

The same day at night, the rest of our company very late returned to the Governor. The one company affirmed, that they had seen in a valley, Eleven Savages, and diverse houses half a mile distant from the steep, or top of the hill where they stayed. The other company had found running out of a high rock, a very fair spring of water, whereof they brought three bottles to the company: for before that time, we drank the stinking water of the pond.

The same second day at night, Captain Stafford, with the Pinnesse, departed from our fleet, riding at Santa Cruz, to an Island called Beake, lying near S Johns, being directed by Ferdinando, who assured him he should there find great plenty of sheep. The next day at night, our planters left Santa Cruz, [5] and came all aboard, and the next morning after, being the 25 of June, we weighed anchor, and departed from Santa Cruz.

The seven and twentieth we came to anchor at Cottea, where we found the Pinnesse riding, at our coming.

The 28 we weighed anchor at Cottea, and presently came to anchor at S. Johns in Musquito bay, where we spent three days unprofitably, in taking in fresh water, spending in the meantime more here, than the quantity of the water came unto.

[5] *With the departure of the pinnace, we can be quite certain the 'planters' travelled on the admiral's ship with John White and Simon Ferdinando and/or on the flyboat, a vessel normally employed as a cargo carrier.*

July

The first we weighed anchor at Mosquito Bay, where were left behind the two Irish men of our company, Darbie Glaven, and Denice Carrell, [6] bearing along the coast of S Johns, till evening, at which time we fell with Rosse bay.

At this place Fernando had promised we should take in salt, and had caused us before, to make and provide as may sacks for that purpose, as we could. The Governor also, for that he understood there was a Town in the bottom of the Bay, not far from the salt hills, appointed thirty shot, ten pikes, and ten targets, to man the Pinnesse, and go aland for salt.

Fernando perceiving them in a readiness, sent to the Governor, using great persuasions with him, not to take in salt there, saying that he knew not well, whether that the same were the place or not: also, that if the Pinnesse went into the Bay, she could not without great danger come back, till the next day at night, and that if in the meantime any storm should rise, the Admiral were in danger to be cast away.

Whilst he was thus persuading, he caused the lead to be cast, and having craftily brought the ship in three fathom, and a half water, he suddenly began to swear, and

---

[6] The spelling of the men's names is given here as written in the account; they are also written elsewhere as Darby Glande and Dennis Carroll.
Footnote: There is a fascinating snippet on Darby Glande's life following his stranding. It is contained in Fray Luis Geronimo de Ore's book 'Relacion de los Martires que ha habido en Florida' written in 1604. In it there is a reference to Darby Glande being a Spanish Galley Slave before being moved to St Augustine where he was noted in 1595.

tear God in pieces, dissembling great danger, crying to him at the helm, bear up hard, bear up hard: so we went off, and were disappointed of our salt, by his means.

The next day, sailing along the West end of S. Johns, the Governor determined to go aland in St Germans Bay, to gather young plants of Oranges, Lemons, Pines, Mameas, and Plantains, to set at Virginia, which we knew might easily be had, for that they grow near the shore, and the places where they grew, well known to the Governor, and some of the planters: [7]

But our Simon denied it, saying: he would come to an anchor at Hispaniola, and there land the Governor, and some other of the Assistants, with the Pinnesse, to see if he could speak with his friend Alanson, of whom he hoped to be furnished both of cattle, and all such things as we would have taken in at S. Johns: but he meant nothing less, as it plainly did appear to us afterwards.

The next day after, being the third of July, we saw Hispaniola, and bear with the coast all that day, looking still when the Pinnesse should be prepared to go for the place where Fernando his friend Alanson was: but that day passed, and we saw no preparation for landing in Hispaniola.

The 4 of July, sailing along the coast of Hispaniola,

[7] *This is evidence that at least some of the personnel on this voyage had previously landed at St Germans. This would appear to confirm that those names that appear on the roster of 1587 were the same individuals as either their namesakes on the 1585 voyage or those who served on the 1586 Drake voyage. They may even possibly have been members of Grenville's 1586 relief voyage (Note: There is no known roster of Grenville's voyage).*

St Germans is recorded in the margin of the original text as being 'A pleasant and fruitful Country, lying on the west end of S. Johns Island where grows plenty of Oranges, Lemons, Plantains and Pines'.

until the next day at noon, and no preparation yet seen for the staying there, we having knowledge that we were past the place where Alanson dwelt, and were come with Isabella: hereupon Fernando was asked by the Governor, whether he meant to speak with Alanson, for the taking in of cattle, and other things, according to his promise or not: but he answered that he was now past the place, and that Sir Walter Raleigh told him, the French Ambassador certified him, that the King of Spain had sent for Alanson into Spain: wherefore he thought him dead, and that it was to no purpose to touch there in any place, at this voyage.

The next day, we left sight of Hispaniola, and hailed off for Virginia, about 4 of the clock in the afternoon.

The sixth of July, we came to the Island Caicos, wherein Fernando said were two salt ponds, assuring us if there were dry, we might find salt to shift with, until the next supply, but it proved as true as the finding of sheep at Beake.

In this Island, whilst Ferdinando solaced himself ashore, with one of the company, in part of the Island, others spent the latter part of that day in other parts of the Island, some to seek the salt ponds, some fowling, some hunting Swans, whereof we caught many. The next day, early in the morning, we weighed anchor, leaving Caicos, with good hope, the first land that we saw next, should be Virginia.

About the 16 of July, we fell with the main of Virginia, which Simon Fernando took to be the Island of Croatoan, where we came to anchor, and rode there two or three days: but finding himself deceived, he weighed, and bear along the coast, where in the night, had not Captain

Stafford been most careful in looking out, then our Simon Fernando, we had been all cast away upon the breach, called the Cape of Fear, for we were come within two cables length [8] upon it: such was the carelessness, and ignorance of our Master.

The two and twentieth of July, we arrived at Hatoraske, where our ship and Pinnesse anchored: the Governor went aboard the Pinnesse, accompanied with forty of his best men, intending to pass up to Roanoke forthwith, hoping there to find those fifteen Englishmen, which Sir Richard Grenville had left there the year before, with whom he meant to have conference, concerning the state of the Country, and Savages, [9] meaning after he had so done, to return again to the fleet, and pass along the coast, to the bay of Chesepiok, where we intended to make our seat and fort, according to the charge given us among other directions in writing, under the hand of Sir Walter Raleigh: [10]

But as soon as we were put with our Pinnesse from the ship, a Gentlemen by the means of Fernando, who was appointed to return for England, called to the sailors in the Pinnesse, charging them not to bring any of the Planters back again, but leave them in the Island, except

[8] 'Two cables length' ~ a cable's length was traditionally the length of the anchor chain (or rope), equivalent to about six hundred feet. Thus the ships came within about twelve hundred feet or four hundred yards of the shore.

[9] John White obviously knew that Grenville had left these men on Roanoke and so must have met with Grenville sometime between 26 December 1586 (Grenville's return) and 26 April 1587. No one else would have been given the instruction to stop over at Roanoke. It is therefore possible that White was resident in Bideford at this time, for we know that Grenville was there building his house on the quayside.

[10] This is confirmation that Roanoke was not the intended location for Raleigh's 'Cittie of Ralegh'.

the Governor, and two or three such as he approved, saying that the summer was far spent, wherefore he would land all the planters in no other place. Unto this were all the sailors, both in the Pinnesse, and ship, persuaded by the Master, wherefore it booted not the Governor to contend with them, but passed to Roanoke, and the same night, at Sunset, went aland on the Island, in the place where our fifteen men were left, but we found none of them, nor any sign, that they had been there, saving only we found the bones of one of those fifteen, which the Savages had slain long before. [11]

The 23 July, the Governor, with diverse of his company, walked to the North End of the Island, where Master Ralfe Lane had his fort, with sundry necessary and decent dwelling houses, made by his men about it the year before, where he hoped to find some signs, or certain knowledge of our fifteen men. When we came thither, we found the fort raised down, [12] but all the houses standing un-burnt, saving the nether rooms of them, and also of the fort, were overgrown with Melons of diverse sorts, and deer within them, feeding on those Melons: so we returned to our company, without hope of ever seeing, any of the fifteen men living.

The same day order was given, that every man should be employed for the repairing of those houses, which we found standing, and also to make other new Cottages, for such as should need.

[11] It is possible the bones they found were not one of the fifteen, but the bones or remains of a hanged man of Lane's colony.
[12] Given the number of men involved in Lane's colony, the present fort declared by the National Park Service to be his is clearly inaccurate. A more likely candidate has recently been identified.

Fernando behaves wickedly

The 25 our fly-boat, and the rest of our planters, arrived all safe at Hatoraske, to the great joy, and comfort of the whole company: but the Master of our Admiral, Fernando grieved greatly at their safe coming: for he purposely left them in the Bay of Portingall, and stole away from them in the night, hoping that the Master thereof, whose name was Edward Spicer, for that he had never been in Virginia, would hardly find the place, or else being left in so dangerous a place as that was, by means of so many men of war, as at that time were aboard, they should surely be taken, or slain: but God disappointed his wicked pretences.

The eighth and twentieth, George Howe, one of our twelve assistants was slain by diverse Savages, which were come over to Roanoke, either of purpose to espy our company, and what number we were, or else to hunt Deer, whereof were many in the Island.

These Savages being secretly hidden among high reeds, where oftentimes they find the Deer asleep, and so kill them, espied our man wading in the water alone, almost naked, without any weapon, save only a small forked stick, catching Crabs therewithal, and also being strayed two miles from his company, shot at him in the water, where they gave him sixteen wounds with their arrows: and after they had slain him with their wooden swords, beat his head in pieces, and fled over the water to the main.

On the thirtieth of July, Master Stafford, and twenty men, passed by water to the Island of Croatoan, with Manteo, who had his mother, and many of his kindred, dwelling in that Island, of whom we hoped to understand some news of our fifteen men, but especially to learn the disposition of the people of the Country towards us, and

Manteo is still their friend.

to renew our old friendship with them. At our first landing, they seemed as though they would fight with us: but perceiving us began to march with our shot towards them, they turned their backs, and fled.

Then Manteo their Countrymen, called to them in their own language, whom as soon as they heard, they returned, and threw away their bows, and arrows, and some of them came unto us, embracing and entertaining us friendly, desiring us not to gather or spill any of their corn, for that they had but little.

We answered them, that neither their corn, nor any other thing of theirs, should be diminished by any of us, and that our coming was only to renew the old love that was between us, and them, at the first, and to live with them as brethren, and friends: which answer seemed to please them well, wherefore they requested us to walk up to their Town, who there seated us after their manner, and desired us earnestly, that there might be some token or badge given them of us, whereby we might know them to be our friends, when we met them anywhere out of the Town or Island.

They told us further, that for want of some such badge, diverse of them were hurt the year before, being found out of an Island by Master Lane his company, whereof they showed us one, which at that very instant lay lame, and had lain of that hurt ever since: but they said, they knew our men mistook them, and hurt them instead of Winginoes men, wherefore they held us excused. [13]

[13] *The only account of a skirmish that Lane gives, other than that encountered on his way to find Chaumis Temoatan, is of one that occurred with Pemisapan. This account therefore suggests either another skirmish went unrecorded or that some of the natives of Croatoan were at Pemisapan's town at the time of Lane's attack.*

August

The next day we had conference further with them, concerning the people of Secota, Aquascogoc, and Pomiok, willing them of Croatoan, to certify the people of those towns, that if they would accept our friendship, we would willingly receive them again, and that all unfriendly dealings past on both parts, should be utterly forgiven, and forgotten.

To this the chief men of Croatoan answered that they would gladly do the best they could, and within seven days, bring the Weroances, and chief Governors of those towns with them, to our Governor at Roanoke, or their answer.

We also understood of the men of Croatoan, that our man Master Howe, was slain by the remnant of Winginoes men, dwelling them at Dasamongueponke, with whom Wanchese kept company: and also we understood by them of Croatoan, how that the 15 Englishmen left at Roanoke the year before, by Sir Richard Grenville, were suddenly set upon by 30 of the men of Secota, Aquascogoc and Dasamongueponke, in manner following.

They conveyed themselves secretly behind the trees, near the houses, where our men carelessly lived: and having perceived that of those 15 they could see but 11 only, two of those Savages appeared to the 11 Englishmen, calling to them by friendly signs, that but two of their chiefest men should come unarmed to speak with those two Savages, who seemed also to be unarmed. Wherefore two of the chiefest of our Englishmen, went gladly to them: but whilst one of those Savages traitorously embraced one of our men, the other with his sword of wood, which he had secretly hidden under his mantle, stroke him on the head, and slew him, and presently, the other eight and twenty Savages showed themselves: the other Englishmen perceiving this fled to his company, whom the Savages pursued with their bows, and arrows, so fast, that the Englishmen were forced to take to the house, wherein all their victual, and weapons were: but the Savages forthwith set the same on fire, by means whereof, our men were forced to take up such weapons as came first to hand, and without order to run forth among the Savages, with whom they skirmished about an hour. In this skirmish, another of our men was shot into the mouth with an arrow, whereof he died: and also one of the Savages was shot into the side by one or our men, with a wildfire arrow, whereof he died presently.

The place where they fought, was of great advantage to the Savages, by means of the thick trees, behind which the Savages through their nimbleness, defended themselves, and so offended our men with their arrows, that our men being some of them hurt, retired fighting to the waterside, where their boat lay, with which they fled towards Hatorask. By that time they had rowed but a quarter of a mile, they espied their four fellows coming from a creek thereby, where they had been to fetch Oysters: these four they received into their boat, leaving Roanoke, and landed on a little Island on the right hand of our entrance into the harbour of Hatorask, where they remained a while. But afterward departed whither, as yet we know not. [14]

[14] This paragraph, if true, means there were thirteen survivors (or sixteen if Diaz was correct). Given that at the time of their arrival (1586) these men would not have known of Raleigh's plan to settle the colony in the Chesapeake Bay region it seems likely that where they went following Hatorask will simply never be known. What we can determine from this account is that the bodies of two of Grenville's men remain undiscovered somewhere on Roanoke.

Having now sufficiently dispatched our business at Croatoan, the same day we departed friendly, taking our leave, and came aboard the fleet at Hatoraske.

The eight of August the Governor having long expected the coming of the Weroances of Pomioake, Aquascogoc Secota, and Dasamongueponke, seeing that the seven days were past, within which they promised to come in, or to send their answers by the men of Croatoan, and no tidings of them heard, being certainly also informed by those men of Croatoan, that the remnant of Wingino his men, which were left alive, who dwelt at Dasamongueponke, were they which had slain George Howe, and were also at the driving of our eleven Englishmen from Roanoke, he thought to defer the revenging thereof no longer. Wherefore the same night, about midnight he passed over the water, accompanied with Captain Stafford, and 24 men, whereof Manteo was one, whom we took with us to be our guide to the place where those Savages dwelt, where he behaved himself toward us as a most faithful Englishman.

The next day being the ninth of August, in the morning so early, that it was yet dark, we landed near the dwelling place of our enemies, and very secretly conveyed ourselves through the woods, to that side, where we had their houses between us and the water: and having espied their fire, and some sitting about it, we presently set on them: the miserable souls herewith amazed, fled into a place of thick reeds, growing fast by, where our men perceiving them, shot one of them through the body with a bullet, and therewith we entered the reeds, among which we hoped to acquire their evil doing towards us, but we were deceived:

for those Savages were our friends, and were come from Croatoan, to gather the corn, and fruit of that place, because they understood our enemies were fled immediately after they had slain George Howe, and for haste had left all their corn, Tobacco, and pompions [15] standing in such sort, that all had been devoured of the birds and the Deer, if it had not been gathered in time: but they had like to have paid dearly for it:

For it was so dark, that they being naked, and their men and women apparelled all so like others, we knew not but that they were all men: and if that one of them, which was a Weroans wife, had not had her child at her back, she had been slain instead of a man, and as hap was, another Savage knew Master Stafford, and ran to him, calling him by his name, whereby he was saved.

Finding ourselves thus disappointed of our purpose, we gathered all the Corn, Peas, Pompions, and Tobacco, that we found ripe, leaving the rest unspoiled, and took Menatoan his wife, with the young child and the other Savages with us over the water to Roanoke. Although the mistaking of these Savages somewhat grieved Manteo, yet he imputed their harm to their own folly, saying to them, that if their Weroans had kept their promise in coming to the Governor, at the day appointed, they had not known that mischance.

The 13 of August, our Savage Manteo, by the commandment of Sir Walter Raleigh, was christened in Roanoke, and called Lord thereof, and of Dasamongueponke, in reward of his faithful service.

[15] 'Pompions' ~ meaning pumpkins or squashes (the English did not discern the difference until the eighteenth century).

The 18 Elenora, [15a] daughter to the Governor, and wife to Ananias Dare, one of the Assistants, was delivered of a daughter in Roanoke, and the same was christened there the Sunday following, and because this child was the first Christian born in Virginia, she was named Virginia.

By this time our ships had unlanded the goods and victuals of the planters and began to take in wood, and fresh water and to new caulk and trim them for England: the planters also prepared their letters, and tokens, to send back into England.

Our two ships, the Lyon and the fly-boat, almost ready to depart, the 21 of August, there arose such a tempest at northeast, that our Admiral then riding out of the harbour, was forced to cut his cables, and put to sea, where he lay beating off and on, six days before he could come to us again, so that we feared he had been cast away, and the rather, for that at the same time that the storm took them, the most, and best of their sailors, were left aland.

At this time some controversies rose between the Governor, and Assistants, about choosing two out of the twelve Assistants, which should go back as factors for the company into England: for every one of them refused, save only one, which all the other thought not sufficient: but at length, by much persuading of the Governor, Christopher Cooper only agreed to go for England: but the next day, through the persuasion of diverse of his familiar friends, he changed his mind, so that now the matter stood as at the first.

The next day, the 22 of August, the whole company,

[15a] 'Elenora' ~ traditionally written as Elinor, but this is the first spelling of her name.

both of the Assistants, and planters, came to the Governor, and with one voice, requested him to return himself into England, for the better and sooner obtaining of supplies, and other necessaries for them: but he refused it, and alleged many sufficient causes, why he would not: the one was, that he could not so suddenly return back again, without his great discredit, leaving the action, and so many, whom he partly had procured through his persuasions, [16] to leave their native Country, and undertake that voyage, and that some enemies to him, and the action at his return into England, would not spare to slander falsely both him, and his action, by saying he went to Virginia, but politically, and to no other end, but to lead so many into a country, in which he never meant to stay himself, and there to leave them behind him.

Also he alleged, that seeing they intended to remove 50 miles further up into the main presently, [17] he being then absent, his stuff, and goods, might be both spoiled, and most of it pilfered away in the carriage so that at his return, he should be either forced to provide himself of

[16] Obviously John White must have canvassed either members of the public, those servants of the known backers of the project, or simply people he knew personally to join him on this voyage.

[17] This is evidence the colonists themselves had obviously been discussing relocation. Yet given the respectable knowledge they had of the area (thanks largely to Lane's voyages of exploration), they would have known that the Chesapeake Bay, the original intended location, was nearly twice that distance; '50 miles' would have been only enough to take them as far north as modern day Currituck, close to the border with Virginia. The alternative theory is that they intended to relocate inland to the area known as Beechlands, an area of sandy hills raised out of the inland swamps on the nearby mainland. The problem with this theory is there is no evidence the colonists would have had any knowledge of these well-hidden inland hills at this time. The area was also considered to be in the hands of Wanchese and natives known to be hostile towards the English settlements. '50 miles' remains a confusing reference.

all such things again, or else at his coming again to Virginia, find himself utterly unfurnished, whereof he had already found some proof, being once from them but three days. [18] Wherefore he concluded, that he would not go himself.

The next day, not only the Assistants, but diverse others, as well women, as men, begun to renew their requests to the Governor again, to take upon him to return into England for the supply, and despatch of all such things, as there were to be done, promising to make him their bond under all their hands, and seals, for the safe preserving of all his goods for him at his return to Virginia, so that if any part thereof were spoiled, or lost, they would see it restored to him, or his assigns, whensoever the same should be missed, and demanded: which bond with a testimony under their hands, and seals, they forthwith made, and delivered into his hands. The copy of the testimony, I thought be good to set down.

"May it please you, her Majesties Subjects of England, we your friends and Countrymen, the planters of Virginia, do by these presents let you, and every of you to understand, that for the present and speedy supply of certain our knowing, and apparent lacks, and needs, most requisite and necessary for the good and happy planting of us, or any others in this land of Virginia, we all of one mind, and consent, have most earnestly entreated, and incessantly requested John White, Governor of the planters in Virginia, to pass into England, for the better and most assured help, and setting forward of the foresaid supplies:

[18] *This seeming-accusation of theft suggests that at least some of the colonists may have had criminal pasts.*

and knowing assuredly that he both can best, and will labour, and take pains in that behalf for us all, and he not once, but often refusing it, for our sakes, and for the honour, and maintenance of the action, hath at last, though much against his will, through our importunacy, yielded to leave his government, and all his goods among us, and himself in all our behalves to pass into England, of whose knowledge, and fidelity in handling this matter, as all others, we do assure ourselves by these presents, and will you to give all credit thereunto, the five and twentieth of August."

The Governor being at the last, through their extreme entreating, constrained to return into England, having then but half a days respite to prepare himself for the same, departed from Roanoke, the seventh and twentieth of August in the morning: and the same day about midnight, came aboard the flyboat, who already had weighed anchor, and rode without the bar, the Admiral riding by them, who but the same morning was newly come thither again.

The same day, both the ships weighed anchor, and set sail for England [19]. At this weighing their anchors, twelve of the men which were in the flyboat, were thrown from the capstan, which by means of a bar that break, came so fast about upon them, that the other two bars thereof stroke and hurt most of them so sore, that some of them never recovered it: nevertheless they assayed presently again to weigh their anchor, but being so weakened with the first fling, they were not able to weigh it, but were

[19] 'Both the ships' ~ this suggests the pinnace remained at Roanoke. Certainly there is no further reference in any documentation relating to Roanoke of Master Edward Stafford nor the pinnace. If they, too, stayed at Roanoke, where is that ship or its remains now?

thrown down, and hurt the second time. Wherefore having in all but fifteen men aboard and most of them by this unfortunate beginning so bruised, and hurt, they were forced to cut their Cable, and leave their anchor.

Nevertheless, they kept company with the Admiral, until the seventeenth of September, at which time we fell with Coruo, and saw Flores.

September

The eighteenth, perceiving of all our fifteen men in the flyboat, there remained but five, which by means of the former mischance, were able to stand to their labour: wherefore understanding that the Admiral meant not to make any haste for England, but linger about the Island of Tercera for purchase, the flyboat departed for England with letters, where we hoped by the help of God to arrive shortly: but by that time we had continued our course homeward, about twenty days, having sometimes scarce, and variable winds, our fresh water also by leaking almost consumed, there arose such a storm at Northeast, which for 6 days ceased not to blow so exceeding:

That we were drawn further in those six than we could recover in thirteen days: in which time others of our sailors began to fall very sick, and two of them died, the weather also continued so close, that our Master sometimes in four days together could see neither Sun nor star, and all the beverage we could make, with stinking water, dregs of beer, and lees of wine which remained, was but three gallons, and therefore now we expected nothing but by famine to perish at sea.

October

The 16 of October we made land, but we knew not what land it was, bearing in with the same land at that day: about Sunset we put into a harbour, were we found a hulk of Dublin, and a pinnesse of Hampton [20] riding, but we knew not as yet what place this was, neither had we any boat to get ashore, until the pinnesse sent off their boat to us with 6 or 8 men of whom we understood we were in Smerwick in the west part of Ireland: they also relieved us presently with fresh water, wine, and other fresh meat.

The 18, the Governor, and the master rode to Dingen Cushe, [21] 5 miles distant, to take order of the new victualing of our flyboat for England, and for relief of our sick and hurt men, but within 4 days after the boatswain, the steward, and the boatswain's mate died aboard the flyboat, and the 28 the Masters mate and tow of our chief sailors were brought sick to Dingen.

November

The first the Governor shipped himself in a ship called

[20] 'Hampton' ~ some sources state that this is Littlehampton, a small port on the Sussex coast, but they are mistaken. 'Hampton' is more correctly identified as the town of Southampton. Littlehampton was known as Hampton but is recorded as changing its name to Littlehampton in 1492 specifically to stop confusion between it and the nearby port of Hampton, which by the 1600s was known as Southampton. This latter port of some four thousand inhabitants had a significant coastal trade in the sixteenth century, while Littlehampton was but a small village of some three hundred inhabitants.
[21] Smerwick is five miles from Dingle, and therefore although this is not positively identifiable, it seems certain that 'Dingen Cushe' means the harbour port of Dingle, Ireland.

the Monkie, which at that time was ready to put to Sea from Dingen for England, leaving the flyboat and all his company in Ireland, the same day we set sail, and on the third day we fell with the Northside of the Lands End, [22] and were shut up by the Severn, [23] but the next day we doubled the same, for Mounts Bay.

The 5 the Governor landed in England at Martasew, [24] near Saint Michaels Mount in Cornwall.

The 8 we arrive at Hampton, where we understood that our consort the Admiral was come to Portsmouth, and had been there three weeks before: and also that Fernando the Master with all his company were not only come home without any purchase, but also in such weakness by sickness, and death of their chiefest men, that they were scarce able to bring their ship into the harbour, but were forced to let fall anchor without, which they could not weigh again, but might all have perished there, if a small bark by great hap had not come to them to help them.

The name of the chief men that died are these, Roger Large, John Mathew, Thomas Smith, and some other their sailors, whose names I know not at the writing hereof. Anno Domini 1587.

The account of the 1587 colony ends with a list of names Hakluyt records as being of the now Lost Colony.

[22] *'Lands End' ~ the most southwesterly point of the British Isles.*
[23] *'Severn' ~ this is a reference to the River Severn, which empties into the Bristol Channel. In the sixteenth century this substantial channel was still referred to as the Severn Estuary.*
[24] *'Martasew' ~ correctly spelled Mousehole (pronounced 'mou-zel'), a small port near Penzance in western Cornwall.*

The names of all the men, women and children, which safely arrived in Virginia, and remained to inhabit there 1587.

Anno Regni Regine Elizabethe 29 [25]

John White
Roger Bailie
Ananias Dare
Christopher Cooper
Thomas Stevens
John Sampson
Dyonis Harvie
Roger Prat
George Howe
Simon Fernando [26]
Nicholas Johnson
Thomas Warner
Anthony Cage
John Jones
John Tydway
Ambrose Viccars
Edmond English
Thomas Topan
Henry Berrye
Richard Berrye
John Spendlove

William Willes
John Brooke
Cutbert White
John Bright
Clement Tayler
William Sole
John Cotsmur
Humfrey Newton
Thomas Colman
Thomas Gramme
Marke Bennet
John Gibbes
John Stilman
Robert Wilkinson
Peter Little
John Wyles
Brian Wyles
George Martyn
Hugh Pattenson
Martyn Sutton
John Farre

[25] *This translates as 'In the 29th year of our Sovereign Queen Elizabeth' i.e. 1587.*
[26] *The presence of Simon Fernando in this list along with John White demonstrates that this list merely records those who stayed on Roanoke during 1587. It is not, as is widely perceived, a list of the 'lost' colonists.*

John Hemmington
Thomas Butler
Edward Powell
John Burden
James Hynde
Thomas Ellis
William Browne
Michael Myllet

Richard Kemme
Thomas Harris
Richard Taverner
John Earnest
Henry Johnson
John Starte
Richard Darige
William Lucas
Arnold Archard
John Wright
William Dutton
Morris Allen
William Waters
Richard Arthur
John Chapman
William Clement
Robert Little
Hugh Tayler

John Bridger
Griffen Jones
Richard Shaberdge
James Lasie
John Cheven
Thomas Hewet
William Berde
Thomas Smith [27]

Women

Elyoner Dare
Margery Harvie
Agnes Wood
Wenefrid Powell
Joyce Archard
Jane Jones
Elizabeth Glane
Jane Pierce
Audry Tappan
Alis Chapman
Emme Merrimoth
Colman
Margaret Lawrence
Joan Warren
Jane Mannering

[27] Of note is that there was a Thomas Smith listed by John White as dying on the return voyage. Given the apparent inaccuracy at [26], this is another of the names appearing on the Lost Colony roster that might or might not have stayed on Roanoke.
NB: Some spellings are slightly different phonetically in the 1600 version, but not enough to cast doubt on whether the people mentioned here are one and the same.

Men (continued)

Richard Wildye
Lewes Wotton
Michael Bishop
Henry Browne
Henry Rufoote
Richard Tomkins
Henry Dorrell
Charles Florrie
Henry Mylton
Henry Payne
William Nicholes
John Borden

Women (continued)

Rose Payne
Elizabeth Viccars

Boys & Children

John Sampson
Robert Ellis
Ambrose Viccars
Thomas Archard
Thomas Humfrey
Tomas Smart
George Howe
John Prat
William Wythers
Thomas Harris
Thomas Phevens
Thomas Scot

Children borne in Virginia

Virginia Dare
Harvye

Savages That were in England and returned home into Virginia with them. Manteo & Towaye

Woman of Pomeiooc carrying a child

Chapter Eight

~

The Voyages of 1588

This chapter is much edited in later editions of Hakluyt's works, yet it provides vital information as to why the small port of Bideford was able to provide such a relatively large fleet to fight the Spanish Armada (see also Chapter One).

The first voyage intended for the supply of the Colonie planted in Virginia by John White which being undertaken in the year 1588 by casualty took no effect.

After the Governors return out of Virginia the 20 of November 1587 he delivered his letters and other advertisements concerning his last voyage and state of the planters to Sir Walter Raleigh: whereupon he forthwith appointed a Pinnesse to be sent thither with all such necessaries as he understood they stood in need of: and also wrote his letters unto them, wherein among other matters he comforted them with promise, that with all convenient speed he would prepare a good supply of shipping and men with sufficient of all things needful, which he intended, God willing, should be with them to Summer following. Which Pinnesse and fleet were accordingly prepared in the West Country at Bideford under the charge of Sir Richard Grenville.

This fleet now being in readiness only staying but for a fair wind to put to sea, at the same time there was spread throughout all England such report of the wonderful preparation and invincible fleets made by the King of Spain joined with the power of the pope for the invading of England, that most of the ships of war then in a readiness in any haven in England were stayed for service at home: And Sir Richard Grenville was personally commanded not to depart out of Cornwall. [1]

The voyage for Virginia by these means for this year thus disappointed, the Governor notwithstanding laboured for the relief of the planters so earnestly, that he obtained two small pinnesses the one of them being of 30 tonnes called the Brave, the other of 25 called the Roe, wherein 15 planters and all their provision, [2] with certain relief for those that wintered in the Country [3] was to be transported.

Thus the 22 of April 1588 we put over the bar at Bideford in the edge of the North side of Cornwall, and the same night we came to an anchor under the Isle of Lundy, where some of the our company went on land: [4]

[1] *Cornwall is incorrect. Bideford is, and has always been, in Devon.*

[2] *Clearly there were a further fifteen people on this voyage intended for the colony. Some reports put this at eleven men and four women but no original documentation appears to be available to confirm this.*

[3] *'In the Country' ~ meaning 'in the country of Virginia'.*

[4] *The date given for departure is five days after Grenville was known to have been in residence at Bideford, having left his fleet to fight the Spanish Armada, with Francis Drake at Plymouth. Did he return to Bideford to see off John White? Lundy Island is twenty miles off the coast from Bideford, and at this date, Grenville owned the island. Its strategic position guarding the entrance to the Bristol Channel would not have been lost on him; perhaps the unusual layover at Lundy was to allow messages to be passed to the island commanders to prepare for the defence of the Channel. We can only hypothesise.*

After we had rode there about the space of three hours we weighed anchor again and all that night we bear along the coast of Cornwall.

The next day being St George's Day and the 23 of April still bearing along the coast we gave chase to 4 ships, and boarded them and forced them all to come to anchor by us in a small bay at the Lands End, out of these ships we took nothing but 3 men and the same night we weighed and put to Sea.

The 24 day we gave chase to 2 ships, the one of them being a Scot and the other a Breton. [5] These we boarded also and took from them whatsoever we could find worth the taking, and so let them go.

The 26 of April we espied a ship on stern of us, for whom we stroke our topsail, and stayed for it. By that time it came with us we saw in his flag a red cross: whereupon we held him for an Englishman, and gave over our preparation to fight with them.

But when he was come near to us we perceived his flag not to be a right St George: whereupon we were somewhat amazed having so far mistaken, for it was a very tall ship, and excellently well appointed and now ready to clap us aboard. [6] And it was not now need to bid every man to bestir himself, for each one prepared with all speed to fight.

In the meantime we hailed them whence they were:

[5] *The boarding of the Scottish and Breton ships is understandable, especially given that the Scots were under the rule of a king friendly to Spain and Rome, and that Breton (Brittany) was annexed to France (another enemy) at this time.*
[6] *'Clap us aboard' ~ meaning to throw grappling irons by which to board the ship.*

They answered of Flushing, bound for Barbary. [7] And they perceiving us to be Englishmen of war bear from us and gave us a piece, and we gave them two pieces [8] and so departed.

The 27 day in the morning we were come with the height of Cape Finisterre, [9] the wind being still at Northeast.

The 28 day the wind shifted: about four of the clock in the afternoon the same day we espied a sail to the weather of us, whom we kept so near unto us as we could all that night.

The 29 in the morning we gave chase to the same ship being then to the wind of us almost as far as we could ken. [9a]

As soon as our Pinnesse, came up to them, the Pinnesse fought with the ship, and it was a hulk of 200 tonnes and more, but after a few great shot bestowed on both sides, the Pinnesse perceiving her consort not able to come to aid her left the hulk and came room with the Brave again.

At their coming they desired the Captain and Master of the Brave to lend them some men and other things whereof they had need.

Which things put aboard them they returned again to the chase of the hulk earnestly, and with full purpose to

7] 'Flushing bound for Barbary' ~ Flushing is a seaport of Holland (Dutch = Vlissingen); Barbary meaning the coast of Africa from Morocco to Libya, an area notoriously linked with the slave trade. We can therefore deduce that this Dutchman was a slave trader.

[8] 'Gave us a Piece' ~ meaning fired a shot. The English response of 'two pieces' suggests this was a mutual exchange to note a truce.

[9] Cape Finisterre ~ the most westerly point of France.

[9a] 'Ken' ~ to understand (Scottish dialect).

board her. But the hulk bear all night in with the coast of Spain, and by morning were so near land, that we fearing either change of wind or to be calmed gave over the fight and put off to Sea again.

May

The first day of May being Wednesday the wind came large at Northeast.

The 3 being Friday we gave chase to another tall ship, but it was night before we spoke with her: and the night grew dark suddenly in such sort, that we lost sight both of the great ship and of our consort also, having thus in the dark lost our Pinnesse, and knowing our Bark so bad of sail that we could neither take nor leave, but were rather to be taken or left of every ship we met, we made our course for the Isle of Madeira, hoping there to find our pinnesse abiding for us.

The same day following being the 5 of May we spoke with a man of war of Rochelle of 60 tonnes, very well manned and bravely appointed being bound, as he said for Peru: having hailed each other, we parted friendly in outward show, giving each other a volley of shot and a great piece: but nevertheless we suspected by which followed: for this Rocheller having taken perfect view of our ship, men and ordinance, towards evening fell on stern of us: and as soon as it was dark left us, and returned to his consort which was a tall ship of 100 tonne lying then on hull to weather of us out of ken, having 84 men in her, whereof 50 were small shot, and 12 muskets, and in the ship 10 pieces of ordinance.

This ship being this night certified by her consort that viewed us, of what force we were and how bad of sail, this greater ship took in 20 of the chiefest men that were in the smaller ship, and presently gave us chase.

The next morning being Monday and the 6 of May, we espied them in the weather of us, so that it was in vain to seek by flight, but rather by fight to help ourselves. The same day about 2 of the clock in the afternoon they were come with us. We hailed them, but they would not answer. Then we waved them to leeward of us, and they waved us with a sword amain, [10] fitting their sails to clap us aboard, which we perceiving gave them one whole side:

With one of our great shot their Master Gunners shoulder was stroke away, and our Master Gunner with a small bullet was shot into the head. Being by this time grappled and aboard each of other the fight continued without ceasing one hour and a half. In which fight were hurt and slain on both sides 23 of the chiefest men, having most of them some 6 or 8 wounds, and some 10 or 12 wounds.

Being thus hurt and spoiled they robbed us of our victuals, powder, weapons and provision, saving a small quantity of biscuit to serve us scarce for England. Our Master and his Mate were deadly wounded, so that they were not able to come forth of their beds.

I myself was wounded twice in the head, once with a sword, and another time with a pike, and hurt also in the side of the buttock with a shot.

[10] 'Amain' ~ an obsolete word meaning 'in a forceful manner'.

Three of our passengers were hurt also, whereof one had 10 or 12 wounds our Master hurt in the face with a pike and thrust quite through the head.

Being thus put to our close fights, and also much pestred with cabbens [11] and unserviceable folks we could not stir to handle our weapons nor charge a piece: again having spent all the powder in our flasks and charges which we had present for our defence, they cut down our netting and entered so many of their men as could stand upon our poop and forecastle, from whence they played extremely upon us with their shot.

As thus we stood resolved to die in fight, the Captain of the Frenchmen cried to us to yield and no force should be offered.

But after we had yielded, they knowing so many of their best men to be hurt and in danger of present death, began to grow into a new fury, in which they would have put us to the sword had not their Captain charged them, and persuaded them to the contrary.

Being at length pacified they fell on all hands to rifling and carrying aboard all the next day until 4 of the clock: at which time by over greedy loading both their own boat and ours, they sunk the one and split the other of the ships side: by means whereof they left us two cables and anchors, all our ordinance and most of our sails, which otherwise had been taken away also.

Furthermore they doubting the wind would arise, and

[11] 'Pestred with cabbens' ~ meaning uncertain. The inference is that the author of the account thought the ship was full of cabins that made it hard to fight effectively.

night at hand, and a tall ship all that day by means of the calm in sight, they came abroad us with their ship, and took in their men that were in us, who left us not at their departing anything worth the carrying away. [12]

Being thus ransacked and used as is aforesaid in all sorts, we determined (as our best shift in so hard a case) to return for England, and caused all our able and unhurt men, to fall to new rigging and mending our sails, tackling, and such things as were spilled in our fight.

By this occasion, God justly punishing our former thievery of our evil disposed mariners, we were of force constrained to break off our intended voyage for the relief of our Colony left the year before in Virginia, and the same night to set our course for England, being than about 50 leagues to the Northeast of Madeira.

The 7 of May being Wednesday in the forenoon the wind came large at East Northeast and we hauled off as far west and north as we could until the 10 of May, fearing to meet with any more men of war, for that we had no manner of weapons left us.

The 11 the wind larged more, and thence forth we continued our due course for England.

The 17 of May we thrust ourselves west of Ushant, and sounded, but found no ground at 110 fathoms. The same day at night we sounded again, and found ground at 80 fathoms.

The 20 being Sunday we fell with the coast of Ireland.

The 21 in the forenoon we saw the Northside of Cornwall at the Lands End.

[12] This is the ship Pedro Diaz, in his deposition at Havana, begged to take him with them.

The 22 of May we came to an anchor between Lundy and Hartland Point near unto Clovelly Quay, where we rode until the next tide, and thence we put over the bar, and the same day landed at Bideford.

Our other Pinnesse whole company we had lost before the last cruel fight, returned also home into Cornwall within a few weeks after our arrival, without performing our intended voyage for the relief of the planters in Virginia, which thereby were not a little distressed.

The Seething of their meals in pots of Earth

Chapter Nine

~

The Deposition of Pedro Diaz 1585-1589

This extraordinary account was discovered some years ago in the Spanish archives and gives us an invaluable insight into the period of Grenville's involvement in the Roanoke voyages from the perspective of one of his captives, held for a time at Bideford.

Pedro de Arana ~
Summary of examination of Pedro Diaz;
Havana, 21 March 1589

[Under date of 26 March 1589, Pedro de Arana forwarded this summary of his examination of Pedro Diaz to the crown through the Spanish Secretary Ybarra, to whom he wrote at the same time.]

In Havana on the twenty-first day of March in the year one thousand five hundred and eighty-nine, Pedro Diaz, resident of La Palma, pilot of this course, furnished the following account as a person whom the English corsairs captured and carried off as he was sailing for Spain in the flagship [1] of the Santo Domingo fleet, commanding, in the year one thousand five hundred and eighty-five.

This vessel was seized in the vicinity of Bermuda by a ship of the queen called the Tyger, under the command of a principal English gentleman named Sir Richard Grenville, the same who in that year was in the island of Puerto Rico and at La Isabella, where he obtained cattle, horses and dogs with which he went to establish a settlement in Florida. [2]

Leaving there a hundred men and cattle, mules and dogs, he sailed thence, and kept informant with him in such manner that he could not escape until the beginning of May, 1588 as follows:

After they captured him in the vicinity of Bermuda they carried informant straight to England by way of the island of Flores. They reached England, port of Plymouth, on November 26, 1585, and the said captain went to London. His home and residence are at Bideford which is on the bar of Barnstaple. [3]

There he equipped six vessels, one of 150 tons and the rest from 100 to 60, and with these and 400 seamen and soldiers and supplies for a year he made sail on May 2, 1586, and steered for Finisterre.

There he encountered fourteen French and Flemish ships out of San Lucar and Cadiz for France and Flanders, of which he captured two. The rest escaped. With these he

[1] The Santa Maria de Vincente.

[2] 'Florida' ~ meaning Virginia; the Spanish in Florida laid claim to the whole of America believing that since they were the first to set foot on it, it was theirs by right.

[3] 'Bar of Barnstaple' ~ this refers to the sandbar that lies across the shared estuary serving the port of Bideford and the town of Barnstaple. It was and remains a danger to shipping.

took a great quantity of merchandise which he sent to his home in the prizes themselves. [3a]

Later he met a Flemish flyboat bound for San Lucar with a cargo of merchandise, and kept this vessel with him after removing its cargo to the six ships of his squadron. He armed this flyboat to fight, for it was a good sailer.

With these seven ships he came up to Porto Santo, an island close to Madeira, and sent a boat to shore to discover conditions there, and to take water and whatever else they might find to hand.

The people there were few but they stood on their defence to prevent the English from landing. They offered to give them a ton of water for each ship, if they would not land. This angered the commander and he attempted to land with the intention of burning and destroying the place and its inhabitants. For this purpose he made ready his boats and ordered his men into them and went to the shore, but the people there prevented him from landing and fought valiantly, in such manner that the Englishman returned to his ships.

Next day he brought his ships close in, to sweep the beach with their artillery. [4] This did the people there little damage because of their defensive works. They held him off until midday, when the Englishman made sail and continued on his course for Florida, where he had left settlers, in latitude 36°. [4a]

[3a] 'Sent to his home' ~ since Grenville was resident at Bideford at this time, this comment implies that these two prizes were dispatched to the port of Bideford. Is it possible that they were renamed to become the Brave and the Roe of 1588?

[4] Whether this incident actually occurred in this detail is not clear from Grenville's account. It is possible that Diaz dramatised it in a manner to protect the Spanish governor from a potential reprisal by the Spanish authorities.

[4a] 'Latitude 36' is a point barely ten miles north of Roanoke and confirms point [2] above.

Beyond Santa Maria Bay the coast runs to the northeast for about 80 leagues to Cape San Juan; from there the coast runs north and south twelve leagues [5] to where this settlement is on an island close to the main. The Island can be crossed on foot. [5a]

The island was inhabited by Indians who were at war with those of the main, for which reason they admitted the English, of whom the mainland Indians killed some four [6] and Francis Drake took the rest away because he found them dispersed and greatly in need of food supplies.

The land produces little to eat. There is only maize and of that little and poor in quality.

And so they found the island deserted; they found an Englishman and an Indian who had been hanged. Of the natives they found only three, and as they were conducting these to their ships two escaped. The other was held prisoner, [7] and of him they learned that Francis Drake had taken away what settlers there were in the island. They have there a timber fort of no great strength, which stands in the water. [7a]

[5] *'Cape San Juan' could be Cape Hatteras, based on the description given here.*
[5a] *A description of Roanoke.*
[6] *This confirms Thomas Cate's account on board Drake's fleet regarding the relief of Lane's colony, wherein he states that 103 Englishmen survived of the 107 recorded as being left there by Grenville.*
[7] *This Indian can be none other than the one that lived at Grenville's house in Bideford. This Indian IS therefore Bideford's Native American known presently only as 'Rawley a Winganditoan' christened according to Bideford parish records on 27 March 1588; after catching an illness that also took Grenville's daughter and one other of his servants, he was buried in St Mary's Parish Churchyard in April 1589.*
[7a] *'In the water' ~ clear evidence that Ralph Lane had set up his fort close to the water's edge, probably almost identical in design and situation to the fort at Tallaboa Bay. This is further confirmation therefore that the present fort on Roanoke Island under the guardianship of the National Park Service and presently marketed as Fort Raleigh is not Lane's fort at Roanoke.*

There is an abundance of timber. The soil is sandy and wet and swampy. Pedro Diaz does not know the quality of the soil of the main, but it seems fertile and heavily wooded. In this fort the Englishman left eighteen men. He would not permit Pedro Diaz to land or to go into the fort. The captain remained there fourteen days: and in the fort were left four pieces of iron ordnance and supplies for the eighteen men for a year. [8] In command of them he left a Master Coffin, Englishman, and another called Chapman. [9]

This Englishman's idea of settling there is that on the main there is a great deal of gold and a waterway from the Atlantic to the Pacific, they say. They think it is nearby, and they intend to establish themselves firmly wherever they find wealth.

This done, the captain made sail with his ships and steered for the open sea, with the intention of encountering vessels from the Indies.

He reached the Azores with his men very sick. About 34 died. From there he crossed to Newfoundland and entered San Francisco Bay where the men went on shore to refresh, and they laid in a supply of fish. [10]

From there he returned to the Azores again, about 400 leagues sailing, and he had been among the islands about

[8] Since Diaz states Grenville would not allow him to land, this makes it certain that not only was Diaz present on the 1586 voyage but that he was present to witness the number of men Grenville left behind. Some credibility therefore has to be given to Diaz's figure of eighteen, not least because Diaz's deposition spells out the word 'eighteen' making the number unmistakable in the account.

[9] Here Diaz also gives us the only known statement providing any names for those men.

[10] This circuitous route is not in Hakluyt's account of the 1585 voyage.

eight days when he took a bark with passengers from San Miguel de la Terceira.

They were humble folk and he carried them along with him and most of them died.

A lad told him that a vessel with a cargo of hides was at an island called Villafranca, where they had unloaded the hides to careen the ship because it leaked. The Englishman went there and carried the hides into his ship.

Off San Miguel he sent a ship to La Terceira which came up to another English vessel which was chasing a frigate from Puerto Rico and together they took her. After which he steered for England where he arrived on December 26, 1586.

He held Pedro Diaz a prisoner, under guard, along with the other Christians he had carried off, about 40 in number. He insisted that only Pedro Diaz knew where that settlement was.

The commander then went to London and raised men for that establishment to the number of 210 persons, men and women, whom he sent out on board of three ships in charge of a Portuguese named Simon Fernandez, married in England, a great pilot and the person who induced them to settle there. [11]

He left for this place in March of 1587, from London, and Pedro Diaz remained incapacitated in the house of the English commander. [12]

[11] *This marriage is not recorded in any known records and therefore cannot be corroborated at the time of writing.*

[12] *The official records state Portsmouth as the point of departure, not London. Since Diaz was, in his own words, 'incapacitated in the house of the English Commander' his statement is not that of an eyewitness. If it is correct, then the colonists would have remained at Portsmouth for around twenty days before sailing for Roanoke, which must be considered unlikely.*

These ships reached the settlement and did not find the eighteen men who had been left there, nor any trace of them. They left the settlers there and returned to England where the English commander made ready two small vessels in which seven men and four women embarked for the said settlement with supplies for them of biscuit, meat and vegetables, with which cargo he sent these vessels out in command of Captain Amadas with Pedro Diaz as pilot. [13]

They proceeded on their voyage and had reached a point some 30 leagues from the island of Madeira when, having sighted a sail, the faster vessel pursued it and so became separated from the other.

The vessel where Pedro Diaz was, continuing on its course, met a French ship which overhauled it, came alongside and sent aboard 30 men with whom the English fought until most of both parties were killed or wounded. The English vessel surrendered to the Frenchman who looted it, removing what he wanted. He left the vessel to some of the English who on their knees begged him to leave Pedro Diaz with them because without him they could not proceed, and would perish. For his part, Pedro Diaz so exerted himself to persuade the Frenchmen not to leave him with the English that he prevailed and the

[13] 'The Commander made ready two small vessels' ~ these were the Brave and the Roe of the 1588 voyage with John White, thus confirming that Grenville left Plymouth just before the Spanish Armada was sighted to return to Bideford to prepare a fleet for John White to return to Roanoke. Diaz's deposition is badly marked at the critical point of naming the commander of the vessels but the best transcription is 'Amayfas'. Surely this is 'Amadas' of the 1584 voyage? Thus, since Diaz was on the Brave and its captain was Arthur Facey, Amadas had to be captain of the Roe. What is also of note is the 'seven men and four women' Diaz quotes as being the colonists on the ill-fated 1588 voyage; Hakluyt describes only fifteen planters.

Frenchman took him with him, promising to set him ashore in the Canaries.

Pedro Diaz escaped from the Frenchman at Isla de Mayo. He reached Havana in the month of March, 1589, where he is at present, intending to go to Spain with the fleet.

Pedro Diaz believes that the settlers of the said establishment will have died of hunger or suffered very grievous want and danger.

Their sitting at meals

Chapter Ten

~

Raleigh's Assignment of 1589

Raleigh's original patent for settling Virginia only granted him seven years to do so. This wordy and complex 'assignment' was clearly his passing over of that charge to those he could trust to continue the work, although after one further voyage they sadly gave up on the work.

An assignment from Sir Walter Raleigh, to divers Gentlemen, and Merchants of London, for the inhabiting, and planting of our people in Virginia

This indenture made the 7 of March in the 31 year [1] of the reign of our Sovereign Lady Elizabeth by the grace of God of England, France, and Ireland Queen, defender of the faith and Country, between the right worshipful Sir Walter Raleigh, of Colaton Raleigh, in the county of Devon knight, Lord warden of the Stannary, and chief governor of Assamacomock alias Wingandacoia, alias Virginia, on the one part, and Thomas Smith, William Sanderson, Walter Bayly, William Gamage, Edmund Nevil,

---

[1] *The thirty-first year of Queen Elizabeth's reign was from 17 November 1588 to 16 November 1589, therefore this indenture was written in 1589.*

158

Thomas Harding, Walter Marler, Thomas Martin, Gabriel Harris, William George, William Stone, Henry Fleetwood, John Gerrard, Robert Macklyn, Richard Hakluyt, Thomas Hoode, Thomas Wade, Richard Wright, Edmund Walden, merchants of London, and adventurers to Virginia aforesaid, John White, Roger Baylye, Ananias Dayre, Christopher Cooper, John Sampson, Thomas Steevens, Roger Prat, Dionise Harvie, John Nichols, Humfrey Dimmocke, [2] late of London Gentlemen, of the other party, witnesseth, that where Sir Walter Raleigh, knight by virtue of the Queens Majesties letters patents dated at Westminster, the 25 day of March in the 26 year of her highness reign, unto him the said Sir Walter Raleigh, by the name of her Majesties trusty, and well-beloved servant, Walter Raleigh Esquire, granted for the discovering, finding out, and planting of unknown and remote lands and countries, as by the said letters patents at large doeth, and may more plainly appear: hath by this indenture of grant bearing date after the computation of England the 7 day of January in the year of our Lord God 1587 and in the 29 year of the reign of our Sovereign Lady Queen Elizabeth, made betwixt him the said Sir Walter Raleigh knight of the one party, and John White, Roger Baylye, Ananias Dayre, Christopher Cooper, John Sampson, Thomas Stevens, William Fulwood, [3] Roger Prat, Dionise Harvie, John

[2] *John Nichols and Humfrey Dimmocke do not appear on Hakluyt's list of 1587 colonists. It is unlikely that Raleigh would have described them as being 'late of London' unless he believed they were in the Virginian colony. Were John Nichols and Humfrey Dimmocke two more 'lost' colonists?*

[3] *William Fulwood, John Nichols, James Plat and Simon Ferdinando are listed in some sources as 'assistants' to John White but excepting the latter, who is known to have returned to England, there is no known record of the whereabouts of the others at the time of this indenture.*

Nichols, [3] George Howe, James Plat, [3] and Simon Ferdinando [3] of London Gentlemen of the other party, granted unto the said John White Roger Baylye, and the rest, free liberty to carry with them into the late discovered barbarous land, and country called Assamacomock, alias Wingandacoia, alias Virginia, there to inhabit with them, such, and so many of her Majesties subjects, as shall willingly accompany them, together with sufficient shipping and furniture for the same, and also diverse, and sundry other prerogatives, jurisdictions, royalties, and pre-eminence's, as in, and by the said indenture of grant, it doeth, and may more at large also appear:

Now the said Thomas Smith, William Sanderson, Walter Baylye, William Gamage, Edmund Nevil, Thomas Harding, Walter Marler, Thomas Martin, Gabriel Harris, William George, William Stone, Henry Fleetwood, John Gerrard, Robert Macklin, Richard Hakluyt, Thomas Hoode, Thomas Wade, Richard Wright, Edmund Walden, and others, adventurers as aforesaid purposing, and intending to be made free of the corporation, company, and society, lately made by the said Sir Walter Raleigh, in the cittie of Ralegh, intended to be erected and builded in Assamacomock, alias Wingandacoia, alias Virginia aforesaid, as by his said indenture made to the said John White, Roger Baylye and the rest more at large it doth appear, do upon my sealing, affecting and confirmation of these patents adventure diverse and sundry sums of money, merchandises, shipping, munition, victual, and other commodities, into the said foreign and remote country of Assamacomock, alias Wingandacoia, alias Virginia aforesaid in confederation as well of which adventure, as also for diverse, and sundry other good causes, and considerations him the said Sir Walter Raleigh thereunto especially moving.

The said Sir Walter Raleigh hath given, granted, covenanted, and promised, and by these presents for himself, his heirs, and assigns and every of them, both give, grant, covenant, and promise, to and with the said Thomas Smith, William Sanderson, Walter Bayly, William Gamage, Edmund Nevil, Thomas Harding, Walter Marler, Thomas Martin, Gabriel Harris, William George, William Stone, Henry Fleetwood, John Gerrard, Robert Machlyn, Richard Hakluyt, Thomas Hoode, Thomas Wade, Richard Wright, Edmund Walden, and others adventurers aforesaid, and unto, and with the said John White, Roger Baylye, Ananias Dayre, Christopher Cooper, John Sampson, Thomas Steevens, Roger Prat, Dionise Harvie, John Nichols, Humfrey Dimmocke, and every of them, their heirs, and assigns, and the heirs and assigns of every of them, and their, and every of their Deputies, Factors, or Apprentices, who shall serve them, or any of them by the space of seven years, that they, and every, or any of them, shall from time to time and at all times for ever have free trade, and traffics for all manner of Merchandise, or commodities whatforever, unto, in, and from all that part of America, called Assamacomock, alias Wingandacoia, alias Virginia aforesaid, or unto, or from any other part, or country of, or in America aforesaid, where he the said Sir Walter Raleigh his heirs or assigns, or any other person or persons claiming or pretending any manner of right, title, or interest, by, from, or under him the said Sir Walter Raleigh, hath, challenged, claimed, or may or shall hereafter, have, challenge, or claim any interest, jurisdiction, title, rule, or privilege, by any convenience, or discovery heretofore made, or hereafter to be made, or by any other way or means whatsoever.

And further the said Sir Walter Raleigh, as well for, and in especial regard, and zeal of planting the Christian religion, in, and amongst the said barbarous and heathen countries, and for the advancement and preferment of the same, and the common utility and profit of the inhabitants therein, as also for the encouragement of the said Thomas Smith, William Sanderson, Walter Bayly, William Gamage, Edmund Nevil, Thomas Harding, Walter Marler, Thomas Martin, Gabriel Harris, William George, William Stone, Henry Fleetwood, John Gerrard, Robert Machlyn, Richard Hakluyt, Thomas Hoode, Thomas Wade, Richard Wright, Edmund Walden, John White, John Nichols, and the other Assistants now lying in Virginia, and others adventurers aforesaid, their heirs, and assigns, both by these presents, freely, and liberally dispose, and give unto them, the said Thomas Smith, William Sanderson and the rest aforesaid, the sum of one hundred pounds of lawful money of England, to be by them adventurers and disposed, in and amongst other their adventures unto the places, and countries before mentioned.

To hath, hold, occupy, use, employ, possess, enjoy, and dispose, as well the said sum of 100 pound, given as aforesaid, as also all such gain, profit, commodity, advantage, and increase, as they by Gods assistance, shall thereof make to their only uses and behoves, and to the uses and behoves of the several heirs, executors, and assigns of them and every of them, without rendering any account for the same, or any parcel thereof, to the said Sir

Walter Raleigh, his heirs, executors or assigns, or any of them. And the said Sir Walter Raleigh, for himself his heirs, and assigns, and every of them, doeth further covenant, and grant, to, and with the said Thomas Smith, William Sanderson, Walter Bayly, William Gamage, Edmund Nevil, Thomas Harding, Walter Marler, and the rest aforesaid, and to, and with the said John White, Roger Baylye, Ananias Dayre, Christopher Cooper, John Sampson, Thomas Steevens, Roger Prat, Dionise Harvie, John Nichols, and Humfrey Dimmocke, and the heirs, and assigns of them, and every of them by these presents, to discharge, save and keep harmless, from time to time, and all times for ever, them, and every of them, their several heirs, and assigns, and every of them, and their deputies, factors and servants of them, and every of them, and apprentices of them, and every or any of them, who shall serve them or any of them the space of seven years, of, and from all rents, subsides, customs, tolls, taxes, tallages, [4] and all other charges, services, duties, and demands, whatsoever required or demanded, or to be required or demanded, at any time or times hereafter, or for the trading, or transporting any commodity or profit, into or from the said country of Assamacomock, alias Wingandacoia, alias Virginia aforesaid, or any other country in America aforesaid, whereunto, or wherein, the said Sir Walter Raleigh, his heirs, or assigns, hath or may or shall have any interest, right or title, by virtue of the said letters patents, or by any discovery, or other means whatsoever, or for any other matter, cause, or thing whatsoever: the

[4] 'Tallages' ~ *meaning occasional other taxes.*

sist [5] part of all the ore of gold, and silver that from time to time, and at all times after such discovery, subduing and possessing as aforesaid, shall there gotten and obtained (always referred to the use of the said Sir Walter Raleigh his heirs, and assigns) only excepted, and fore prised.

And the said Sir Walter Raleigh doeth further covenant, and grant by these presents for him, his heirs, and assigns, to and with the said Thomas Smith, William Sanderson, and the rest aforesaid their heirs and assigns, that he the said Sir Walter Raleigh, his heirs, or assigns, upon sufficient and reasonable request made to him by the persons aforesaid, or any of them, their heirs, or assigns, shall and will at any time, or times hereafter, ratify, affirm, and approve by his deed, or deeds, or by any other conveyance, or conveyances in law, the corporation heretofore made by him the said Sir Walter Raleigh, consisting of one Governor, and twelve assistants, as by his said Indenture made to John White and others, more plainly doth appear, for the more perfect, and better assurance, and sure making of the said corporation, if any imperfection, and want in law thereof be. And further, that he the said Sir Walter Raleigh, his heirs, and assigns, shall, and will, as much as in him or them lieth, procure, and endeavour to obtain, the Queens majesties letters patents, for ratification, approbation, and more sure confirmation, of the said corporation, and society with all prerogatives, commodities, jurisdictions, royalties, privileges, and pre-eminences, whatsoever granted, and covered by her Majesty, to the said Sir Walter Raleigh, his heirs or assigns, or by him the

[5] 'Sist' ~ a Scottish term meaning to summon or to bring forth.

said Sir Walter Raleigh, to the said John White, and others, as by his said indenture of grant made to the said John White, and others more plainly appeared.

In witness whereof, the parties to these presents, have hereunto interchangeably put their hands, and seals, the day and year first above written.

Indian village of Secotan

Chapter Eleven

~

The Voyage of 1590

This final account is taken from the 1600 edition of Hakluyt's narrative and details the final attempt to find the Lost Colony, there being no further effort for more than four hundred years.

The fifth voyage of M. John White into the West Indies and parts of America called Virginia in the year 1590.

The 20 of March the three ships the Hopewell, the John Evangelist, and the Little John, put to Sea from Plymouth with two small Shallops. [1]

The 25 at midnight both our Shallops were sunk being towed at the ships sterns by the Boatswains negligence.

On the 30 we saw ahead us that part of the coast of barbary, lying East of Cape Cantyn, and the Bay of Asaphi.

The next day we came to the Isle of Mogador, [2] where rode, at our passing by, a Pinnesse of London called the Moonshine.

[1] 'Shallop' ~ a small open boat usually fitted out with oars and one or two masts; it would not have been dissimilar to a modern-day yacht.
[2] The Isle of Mogador is a small island in the harbour of Essaouira, Morocco (Essaouira formerly being called Mogador).

April

On the first of April we anchored in Santa Cruz road, where we found two great ships of London lading with Sugar, of whom we had 2 shipboats to supply the loss of our Shallops.

On the 2 we set sail from the road of Santa Cruz, for the Canaries.

On Saturday 4 we saw Alegranza, the East Isle of the Canaries.

On Sunday 5 of April we gave chase to a double flyboat, the which, we also the same day fought with, and took her, with loss of three of their men slain, and one hurt.

On Monday the 6 we saw Grand Canary, and the next day we landed and took in fresh water on the Southside thereof.

On the 9 we departed from Grand Canary, and framed our course for Dominica.

The last of April we saw Dominica, and the same night we came to an anchor on the Southside thereof.

May

The first of May in the morning many of the Savages came aboard our ships in their canoes, and did traffic with us: we also the same day landed and entered their Town from whence we returned the same day aboard without any resistance of the Savages; or any offence done to them.

The 2 of May our Admiral and our Pinnesse departed from Dominica leaving the John our Vice-admiral playing off and on about Dominica, hoping to take some Spaniard outwards bound to the Indies; the same night we had sight of three small Islands called Los Santos, leaving Guadalope and them on our starboard.

The 3 we had sight of St Christophers Island, bearing Northeast and East of us.

On the 4 we sailed by the Virgins, [3] which are many broken Islands, lying at the East end of St John's Island; and the same day towards evening we landed upon on of them called Blanca, where we killed an incredible number of fowls: here we stayed but three hours, and from thence stood into the shore Northwest, and having brought this Island Southeast off us, we put towards night through an opening or swatch, called The passage, lying between the Virgins, and the East end of St John: here the Pinnesse left us and sailed Southside of St John.

The 5 and 6 the Admiral sailed along the Northside of St John, so near the shore that the Spaniards discerned us to be men of war; and therefore made fires along the coast as we sailed by, for so their custom is, when they see any men of war on their coasts.

The 7 we landed on the Northwest end of St John, where we watered in a good river called Yaguana, and the same night following we took a Frigate of ten Tunne coming from Gwathanelo laden with hides and ginger. In

[3] 'Virgins' ~ Virgin Islands.

this place Pedro a Mollato, who knew all our state, ran from us to the Spaniards. [4]

On the 9 we departed from Yaguana.

The 13 we landed on an Island called Mona, whereon were 10 or 12 houses inhabited of the Spaniards; these we burned and took from them a Pinnesse, which they had drawn aground and sunk, and carried all her sails, masts, and rudders into the woods, because we should not take him away; we also chased the Spaniards over all the Island; but they hid them in caves, hollow rocks, and bushes, so that we could not find them.

On the 14 we departed from Mona, and the next day after we came to an island called Saona, about 5 leagues distant from Mona, lying on the Southside of Hispaniola near the East end: between these two Islands we lay off and on 4 or 5 days, hoping to take some of the Domingo fleet doubling this Island, as a nearer way to Spain than by Cape Tyburon, or by Cape St Anthony.

On Thursday being the 19 our Vice-admiral, from whom we departed at Dominica, came to us at Saona, with whom we left a Spanish Frigate, and appointed him to lie off and on another five days between Saona and Mona to the end aforesaid; then we departed from them at Saona for Cape Tyburon, Here I was informed that our men of the Vice-admiral, at their departure from Dominica brought away two young Savages, which were the chief Casiques

[4] *This suggests that 'Pedro a Mollato' ('mulatto' meaning he was of mixed race, not that Mollato was his surname) was a member of the crew of the Hopewell. It is reasonable to assume that he was also a Spanish pilot held captive by the English. This is a remarkably similar situation to that of Pedro Diaz, who was taken prisoner by Grenville in 1585 and escaped in White's ill-fated 1588 voyage. Since it is recorded that Grenville held two Spanish pilots captive, could this Pedro be the second?*

sons of that Country and part of Dominica, but they shortly after ran away from them at Santa Cruz Island where the Vice-admiral landed to take in ballast.

On the 21 the Admiral came to the Cape Tyburon, where we found the John Evangelist our Pinnesse staying for us: here we took in two Spaniards almost starved on the shore, who made a fire to our ships as we passed by. Those places for an 100 miles in length are nothing else but a desolate and wilderness, without any habitation of people, and full of wild Bulls and Boars, and great Serpents.

The 22 our Pinnesse came also to an anchor in Alligator Bay at Cape Tyburon. Here we understood of M. Lane Captain of the Pinnesse; how he was set upon with one of the kings Galleys belonging to Santo Domingo, which was manned with 400 men, who after he had fought with him 3 or 4 hours, gave over the fight and forsook him, without any great hurt done on either part.

The 26 The John our Vice-admiral came to us to Cape Tyburon, and the Frigate which we left with him at Saona. This was the appointed place which we should attend for the meeting with the Santo Domingo fleet.

On Whitsunday eve at Cape Tyburon one of our boys ran away from us, and at ten days end returned to our ships almost starved for want of food. In sundry places about this part of Cape Tyburon we found the bones and carcasses of diverse men, who had perished (as we thought) by famine in those woods, being either straggled from their company, or landed there by some men of war.

June

On the 14 of June we took a small Spanish frigate which fell amongst us so suddenly, as he doubled the point at the Bay of Cape Tyburon, where we rode, so that he could not escape us. This frigate came from Santo Domingo, and had but 3 men in her, the one was an expert Pilot, the other a Mountaineer, and the third a Vintner, who escaped all out of prison at Santo Domingo, purposing to fly to Yaguana which is a town in the West parts of Hispaniola where many fugitive Spaniards are gathered together.

The 17 being Wednesday Captain Lane was sent to Yaguana with his Pinnesse and a Frigate to take a ship, which was there taking in freight, as we understood by the old Pilot, whom we had taken three days before.

The 24 the Frigate returned from Captain Lane at Yaguana, and brought us word to Cape Tyburon, that Captain Lane had taken the ship, with many passengers and Negroes in the same: which proved not so rich a prize as we hoped for, for that a Frenchman of war had taken and spoiled her before we came. Nevertheless her loading was thought worth 1000 or 1300 pounds, being hides, ginger, Cannafistula, [5] Copper pans, and Cassava.

July

The second of July Edward Spicer whom we left in England came to us at Cape Tyburon, accompanied with a small

[5] *'Cannafistula' ~ cassia tree, the bark of which had a medicinal value.*

Pinnesse, whereof one M. Harps was Captain. And the same day we had sight of a fleet of 14 sail all of Santo Domingo, to whom we presently gave chase, but they upon the first sight of us fled, and separating themselves scattered here and there: Wherefore we were forced to divide ourselves and so made after them until 12 of the clock at night.

But then by reason of the darkness we lost sight of each other, yet in the end the Admiral and the Moonelight happened to be together the same night at the fetching up of the Vice-admiral of the Spanish fleet, against whom the next morning we fought and took him, with loss of one of our men and two hurt, and of theirs 4 slain and 6 hurt.

But what was become of our Vice-admiral, our Pinnesse, and Prize, and two Frigates, in all this time, we were ignorant.

The 3 of July we spent about rifling, rummaging and fitting the Prize to be sailed with us.

The 6 of July we saw Jamaica the which we left on our larboard, keeping Cuba in sight on our starboard.

Upon the 8 of July we saw the Island of Pinos, which lieth on the Southside of Cuba nigh unto the West end or Cape called Cape St Anthony. And the same day we gave chase to a Frigate, but at night we lost sight of her, partly by the slow sailing of our Admiral, and lack of the Moonelight our Pinnesse, whom Captain Cooke had sent to the Cape the day before.

On the 11 we came to Cape St. Anthony, where we found our consort the Moonelight and her Pinnesse abiding for our coming, of whom we understood that the day before there passed by them 22 sail, some of them of the burden of 300 and some 400 tunnes laden with the Kings treasure from the main, bound for Havana; from this 11 of July until 22 we were much becalmed: and the wind being very scarce, and the weather exceeding boat, we were much pestered with the Spaniards we had taken: wherefore we were driven to land all the Spaniards saving three, but the place where we landed them was of their own choice on the Southside of Cuba near unto the Organes and Rio de Puercos.

The 23 we had sight of the Cape of Florida, and the broken Islands thereof called the Martires.

The 25 being St James day in the morning we fell with the Matancas, a head-land 8 leagues towards the East of Havana, where we purposed to take fresh water in, and make our abode two of three days.

On Sunday the 26 of July plying too and fro between the Matancas and Havana, we were espied of three small Pinnesses of St John de Ullua bound for Havana, which were exceeding richly laden.

These 3 Pinnesses came very boldly up unto us, and so continued until they came within musket shot of us. And we supposed them to be Captain Harp's pinnesse, and two small Frigates taken by Captain Harpe: wherefore we showed our flag.

But they presently upon the sight of it turned about and made all the sail they could from us toward the shore, and kept themselves in so shallow water, that we were not able to follow them, and therefore gave them over with expense of shot and powder to no purpose.

But if we had not so rashly set out our flag, we might have taken them all three, for they would not have known us before they had been in our hands.

This chase brought us so far to leeward as Havana: wherefore not finding any of our consorts at the Matancas, we put over again to the Cape of Florida, and from thence through the channel of Bahama.

On the 28 the Cape of Florida bare West of us.

The 30 we lost sight of the coast of Florida, and stood to Sea for to gain the help of the current which ruinneth much swifter afar off than in sight of the coast. For from the Cape to Virginia all along the shore are none but eddy currents, setting to the South and Southwest.

The 31 our three ships were clearly disbocked, the great prize, the Admiral, and the Mooneshine, but our prize being thus disbocked departed from us without taking leave of our Admiral or consort, and sailed directly for England.

August

On the first of August the wind scanted, and from thence forward we had very foul weather with much rain, thundering, and great spouts, which fell round about us nigh unto our ships.

The 3 we stood again in for the shore, and at midday we took the height of the same. The height of that place we found to be 34 degrees of latitude.

Towards night we were within three leagues of the Low sandy Islands West of Wokokon. [6] But the weather

---

[6] 'Low sandy Islands' ~ what is known today as Portsmouth Island.

continued so exceeding foul, that we could not come to an anchor near the coast: wherefore we stood off again to Sea until Monday the 9 of August.

On Monday the storm ceased and we had very great likelihood of fair weather: therefore we stood in again for the shore: and came to an anchor at 11 fathom in 35 degrees of Latitude, [6a] within a mile of shore, where we went on land on the narrow sandy Island, being one of the Islands West of Wokokon: in this Island we took in some fresh water and caught great store of fish in the shallow water. Between the main (as we supposed) and that Island it was but a mile over and three or four feet deep in most places.

On the 12 in the morning we departed from thence and towards night we came to an anchor at the Northeast end of the Island of Croatoan, by reason of a breach which we perceived to lie out two or three leagues into the Sea: here we rode all that night.

The 13 in the morning before we weighed our anchors, our boats were sent to found over this breach; our ships riding on the side thereof at 5 fathoms; and a ships length from us we found but 4 and a quarter, and then deeping and shallowing for the space of two miles, so that sometimes we found 5 fathom, and by and by 7, and within two casts with the lead 9, and then 8, next cast 5, and then 6, and then 4, and then 9 again, and deeper; but 3 fathom was the least, 2 leagues off from the shore.

This breach is in 35 degree and a half, and lieth at the

[6a] *The northern tip of Portsmouth Island, confirmed by the following sentence, which states 'one of the islands west of Wokokon (Ocracoke)'.*

very Northeast point of Croatoan, whereas goes a fret out of the main Sea into the inner waters, which part the Islands and the mainland. [7]

The 15 of August towards Evening we came to an anchor at Hatorask, in 36 degrees and one-third, in five fathoms of water, three leagues from the shore. At our first coming to anchor on this shore we saw a great smoke rise in the Isle Roanoke near the place where I left our Colony in the year 1587, which smoke put us in good hope that some of the Colony were there expecting my return out of England.

The 16 and next morning our 2 boats went ashore, and Captain Cooke, and Captain Spicer, and their company with me, with intent to pass at Roanoke where our countrymen were left. At our putting from the ship we commanded our master gunner to make ready 2 Minions and a Falcon well loaded, and to shoot them off with reasonable space between every shot, to the end that their reports might be heard to the place where we hoped to find some of our people. This was accordingly performed, and our two boats put off unto the shore, in the Admirals boat we sounded all the way and found from our ship until we came within a mile of the shoreline, eight, and seven fathom: but before we were halfway between our ships and

---

[7] This detailed description of the breach has usually been described as one of the 'false capes' known to have existed south of Hatorask around Pea Island today. However, given the accuracy of Elizabethan navigation at this time, the latitude stated here places the ships just north of Avon on what is Hatteras Island today. This means that White could have been describing the breach he drew on his map of the period, just north of modern Buxton, five miles south of Avon. If this is the case, then as White's men passed through that breach, they may have been within a few hundred yards of spotting native Croatoan Indians or possibly even his colony, if they did indeed relocate to the island.

the shore we saw another great smoke to the Southwest of Kindrikers Mounts: [8] we therefore thought good to go to that second smoke first: but it was much further from the harbour where we landed, than we supposed it to be, so that we were very sore tired before we came to the smoke.

But that which grieved us more was that when we came to the smoke, we found no man for sign that any had been there lately, nor yet any fresh water in all this way to drink. Being thus weary with this journey we returned to the harbour where we left our boats, who in our absence had brought their cask ashore for fresh water, so we deferred our going to Roanoke until the next morning, and caused some of those sailors to dig in those sandy hills for fresh water whereof we found very sufficient.
That night we returned aboard with our boats and one whole company in safety.

The next morning being the 17 of August, our boats and company were prepared again to go up to Roanoke, but Captain Spicer had then sent his boat ashore for fresh water, be means whereof it was ten of the clock afore noon before we put from our ships which were then come to an anchor within two miles of shore.

The Admirals boat was halfway towards the shore, when Captain Spicer put off from his ship. The Admirals boat first passed to the breach, but not without some danger of sinking, for we had a sea break into our boat which filled us half full of water, but by the will of God and careful

[8] 'Kindrikers Mounts' ~ this is thought to be a sand dune area near modern-day Wimble Shoals north of Rodanthe, although some authorities dispute this, stating that it could be what is now Kill Devil Hills, some way north of Roanoke. Given the latitude quoted by White and the direction 'southwest', this is not possible.

steerage of Captain Cooke we came safe ashore, saving only that our furniture, victuals, match and powder were much wet and spoiled.

For at this time the wind blew at Northeast and direct into the harbour so great a gale, that the Sea broke extremely on the bar, and the tide went very forcibly at the entrance. By that time our Admirals boat was hauled ashore, and most of our things taken out to dry, Captain Spicer came to the entrance of the breach with his mast standing up, and was half passed over, but by the rash and indifferent steerage of Ralph Skinner his Masters mate, a very dangerous Sea broke into their boat and overset them quite, the men kept the boat some in it, and some hanging on it, but the next sea set the boat on ground, where it beat so, that some of them were forced to let go their hold, hoping to wade ashore, but the Sea still beat them down, so that they could neither stand nor swim, and the boat twice or thrice was turned the keel upward, whereon Captain Spicer and Skinner, hung until they sunk, and were seen no more.

But four that could swim a little kept themselves in deeper water and were saved by Captain Cooke's means, who so soon as he saw their oversetting, stripped himself, and four other that could swim very well, and with all haste possible rowed unto them, and saved four.

They were 11 in all, and 7 of their chiefest were drowned, whose names were Captain Edward Spicer, Ralph Skinner, Edward Kelley, Thomas Bevis, Hance the Surgeon, [8a] Edward Kelborne, Robert Coleman.

[8a] 'Hance the Surgeon' ~ Haunce Walters of the 1585 voyage?

This mischance did so much discomfort the sailors, that they were all of a one mind not to go any further to seek the planters.

But in the end by the commandment and persuasion of me and Captain Cooke, they prepared the boats: and seeing the Captain and me so resolute, they seemed much more willing. Our boats and all things fitted again, we put off from Hatorask, being the number of 19 persons in both boats: but before we could get to the place, where our planters were left, it was so exceeding dark, that we overshot the place a quarter of a mile: there we espied towards the North end of the Island by light of a great fire through the woods, to the which we presently rowed: when we came right over against it, we let fall our Grapnel near the shore, and sounded with a trumpet a Call and afterwards many familiar English tunes of Songs, and called to them friendly; but we had no answer, we therefore landed at daybreak, and coming to the fire, we found the grass and sundry rotten trees burning about the place.

From hence we went through the woods to that part of the Island directly over against Dasamongwepenk, and from thence we returned b the waterside, round about the North point of the Island, until we came to the place where I left our Colony in the year 1586. [9]

In all this way we saw in the sand the print of the Savages feet of 2 or 3 sorts trodden by night, and we entered up the sandy bank upon a tree, in the very brow thereof were curiously carved there fair Roman letters C R O: which letters presently we knew to signify the place,

[9] 1586 is in error. The date should be 1587.

where I should find the planters seated, according to a secret token agreed upon between them and me at my last departure from them, which was, that in any ways they should not fail to write or carve on the trees or posts of the doors the name of the place where they should be seated; for at my coming away they were prepared to remove from Roanoke 50 miles into the main. [9a]

Therefore at my departure from them in An.1587 I willed them, that if they should happen to be distressed in any of those places, that then they should carve over the letters or name, a Cross + in this form, but we found no such sign of distress. And having well considered of this, we passed towards the place where they were left in sundry houses, but we found the houses taken down, and the place very strongly enclosed with a high palisade of great trees, with cortynes [10] and flankers very fort-like, and one of the chief trees or posts at the right side of the entrance had the bark taken off, and 5 foot from the ground in fair Capital letters was graven C R O A T O A N without any cross or sign of distress; this done, we entered into the palisade, where we found many bars of Iron, two pigs of Lead, four ironfowlers, Iron sacket-shot, and such

---

[9a] *A reference consistent with White's statement made in 1587 at the point of his leaving the colony. 'Main' could be inferred to mean fifty miles into the Spanish Main, meaning heading fifty miles south towards Spanish-held territory. This would make sense of White's avid expression that he felt Croatoan Island was where his colonists were (being fifty miles south or fifty miles into the main).*

[10] *'Cortynes' ~ meaning slots for looking through, as in a knight's helmet.*

like heavy things, thrown here and there, almost overgrown with grass and weeds. [11]

From thence we went along by the water side, towards the point of the Creek to see if we could find any of their boats or Pinnesse, but we could perceive no sign of them, nor any of the last Falcons and small Ordnance which were left with them, at my departure from them.

At our return from the Creek, some of our Sailors meeting us, told us that they had found where diverse chests had been hidden, and long since digged up again and broken up, and much of the goods in them spoiled and scattered about, but nothing left, of such things as the Savages knew any use of, undefaced.

Presently Captain Cooke and I went to the place, which was in the end of an old trench, made two years past by Captain Amadas: [12] where we found five chests, that had been carefully hidden of the Planters, and of the same chests three were my own, and about the place many of my things spoile and broken, and my books torn from the

---

[11] *Since John White was present in 1585 when the military colony was stationed on Roanoke, he would have detailed knowledge of the fort that Ralph Lane built. Here, he notes with some surprise how much more strengthened the fort is and the significant amount of iron workings that had taken place within. This suggests strongly that the colonists must have stayed for some while in order to complete the work they did, and it also suggests that they feared or suffered from attacks, probably from Wanchese's men or those friendly to his cause.*

[12] *Amadas was captain of the Roe two years previously. If this statement is correct then Amadas made it to Roanoke in 1588. The 1588 account states, though, that Amadas arrived back at Bideford without having relieved the colony. Could this mean he never made it to Roanoke or that he actually did, but upon not finding the colony there, simply left? Most likely the date is inaccurate, but in considering this we must therefore accept that Amadas was a member of the 1587 voyage even though his name is not recorded as a captain of any of the vessels, nor referred to in any of White's narrative from that voyage.*

covers, the frames of some of my pictures and Maps rotten and spoiled with rain, and my armour almost eaten through with rust; this could be no other but the deed of the Savages our enemies at Dasamongwepeuk, who had watched the departure of our men to Croatoan; and as soon as they were departed, digged up every place where they suspected any thing to be buried: but although it much grieved me to see such spoil of my goods, yet on the other side I greatly joyed that I had safely found a certain token of the safe being at Croatoan, which is the place where Manteo was born, and the Savages of the island our friends.

When we had seen in this place so much as we could, we returned to our boats, and departed from the shore towards our Ships, with as much speed as we could: For the weather began to overcast, and very likely that a foul and stormy night would ensue.

Therefore the same Evening with much danger and labour, we got ourselves aboard, by which time the wind and seas were so greatly risen, that we doubted our cables and Anchors would scarcely hold until Morning; where fore the Captain caused the Boat to be manned with five lusty men, who could swim all well, and sent them to the little Island on the right hand of the Harbour, to bring aboard five of our men, who had filled our cask with fresh water: the Boat the same night returned aboard with our men, but all our Cask ready filled they left behind, impossible to be had aboard without danger of casting away both men and Boats; for this night proved very stormy and foul.

The next Morning it was agreed by the Captain and

myself, with the Master and others, to weigh anchor, and go for the place at Croatoan, where our planters were: for that then the wind was good for that place, and also to leave that Cask with fresh water on shore in the Island until our return. So then they brought the cable to the Capstan, but when the Anchor was almost on deck, the cable broke, by means whereof we lost another Anchor, where with we drove so fast ashore, that we were forced to let fall a third Anchor; which came so fast home the Ship was almost aground by Kendricks Mounts: so that we were forced to let slip the Cable end for end. And if it had not chanced that we had fallen into a channel of deeper water, closer by the shore then we accompted [13] of, we could never have gone clear of the point that lyeth to the Southwards of Kenricks mounts.

Being this clear of some dangers, and gotten into deeper waters, but not without some loss; for we had but one Cable and Anchor left us of four, and the weather grew to be fouler and fouler; our victuals scarce, and our cask and fresh water lost: it was therefore determined that we should go for Saint John or some other Island to the Southward for fresh water.

And it was further purposed, that if we could any ways supply our wants of victuals and other necessaries, either at Hispaniola, Saint John, or Trinidad, that then we should continue in the Indies all the Winter following, with hope to make 2 rich voyages of one, and at our return to visit our countrymen at Virginia.

The captain and the whole company in the Admiral

[13] 'Accompted' ~ meaning 'accounted'.

(with my earnest petitions) thereunto agreed, so that it rested only to know what the Master of the Moonelight our consort would do herein. But when we demanded them if they would accompany us in that new determination, they alleged that their weak and leaky Ship was not able to continue it; wherefore the same night we parted, leaving the Moonelight to go directly for England, and the Admiral set his course for Trinidad, which course we kept two days.

On the 28 the wind changed, and it was set on foul weather every way: but this storm brought the wind West and Northwest, and blew so forcibly, that we were able to bear no sail, but our fore-course half mast high, wherewith we ran upon the wind perforce, the due course for England, for that we were driven to change our first determination for Trinidad, and stood for the Islands of Azores, where we purposed to take in fresh water, and also there hoped to meet with some English men of war about those Islands, as whose hands we might obtain some supply of our wants.

September

And thus continuing our course for the Azores, sometimes with calms, and sometimes with very scarce winds, on the fifteenth of September the winds came South Southeast, and blew so exceedingly, that we were forced to lie atry all that day.

At this time by account we judged ourselves to be about twenty leagues to the West of Cuerno and Flores, but about night the storm ceased, and fair weather ensued. On Thursday the seventeenth we saw Cuerno and Flores, but we could not come to an anchor that night, by reason the wind shifted.

The next Morning being the eighteenth, standing in again with Cuerno, we espied a sail ahead us, to whom we gave chase: but when we came near him, we knew him to be a Spaniard; and hoped to make sure purchase of him; but we understood at our speaking with him, that he was a prize, and of the Domingo fleet already taken by the John our consort, in the Indies.

We learned also of this prize, that our Vice-admiral and Pinnesse had fought with the rest of the Domingo fleet, and had forced them with their Admiral to flee unto Jamaica under the Fort for succour, and some of them ran themselves aground, whereof one of them they brought away, and took out of some others so much as the time would permit.

And further we understood of them; that in their return from Jamaica about the Organes near Cape Saint Anthony, our Vice-admiral met with two Ships of the mainland, come from Mexico, bound for Havana, with whom he fought; in which fight our Vice-admirals Lieutenant was slain, and the Captains right arm stroke off, with four other of his men slain, and fifteen hurt.

But in the end he entered, and took one of the Spanish ships, which was so sore shot by us under water, that before they could take out her treasure, she sunk; so that we lost thirteen Pipes of silver which sunk with her, besides much other rich merchandise. And in the meantime the other Spanish ship being pierced with nine shot under water, got away; whom our Vice-admiral intended to pursue: but some of their men in the top made certain rocks, which they saw above water near the shore, to be Galleys of Havana and Cartegena, coming from Havana to rescue the two Ships; Wherefore they gave over their chase, and went for England.

After this intelligence was given us by this our prize, he departed from us, and went for England.

On Saturday the 19 of September we came to an anchor near a small village on the North side of Flores, where we found riding 5 English men of war, of whom we understood that our Vice-admiral and Prize were gone thence for England. One of these five was the Moonelight our consort, who upon the first sight of our coming into Flores, set sail and went for England, not taking any leave of us.

On Sunday the 20 the Mary Rose, Admiral of the Queens fleet, wherein was General Sir John Hawkins, stood in with Flores, and diverse other of the Queens ships, namely the Hope, the Nonpareilia, the Rainbow, the Swiftsure, the Foresight, with many other good merchants ships of war, as the Edward Bonaventure, the Merchant Royal, the Amitie, the Eagle, the Dainty of Sir John Hawkins, and many other good ships and Pinnesses, all attending to meet with the King of Spain's fleet, coming from Terra firma of the West Indies.

The 22 of September we went aboard the Rainbow, and towards night we spoke with the Swiftsure, and gave him 3 pieces. The captains desired our company; wherefore we willingly attended on them: who at this time with 10 other ships stood for Faial. But the General with the rest of the Fleet were separated from us, making two fleets, for the surer meeting with the Spanish fleet.

On Wednesday the 23 we saw Gratiosa, where the Admiral and the rest of the Queens fleet were come together. The Admiral put forth a flag of counsel, in which was determined that the whole fleet should go for the main, and spread themselves on the coast of Spain and Portugal, so far as conveniently they might, for the surer meeting of the Spanish fleet in those parts.

The 26 we came to Faial, where the Admiral with some other of the fleet anchored, othersome plied up and down between that and the Pico until midnight, at which time the Antony shot off a piece and weighed, showing his light: after whom the whole fleet stood to the East, the wind at Northeast by East.

On Sunday the 27 towards Evening we took our leave of the Admiral and the whole fleet, who stood to the East. But our ship accompanied with a Flyboat stood in again with St George, where we purposed to take in more fresh water, and some other fresh victuals.

On Wednesday the 30 of September, seeing the wind hang so Northerly, that we could not attain the Island of St George, we gave over our purpose to water there, and the next day framed our due course for England.

October

The 2 of October in the Morning we saw St Michaels Island on our Starboard quarter.

The 23 at 10 of the clock afore noon, we saw Ushant in Brittany.

On Saturday the 24 we came in safety, God be thanked, to an anchor at Plymouth.

* * *

The above transcript was submitted by John White three years after the voyage. With it came the following letter:

To the Worshipful and my very friend Master Richard Hakluyt, much happiness in the Lord

Sir, as well for the satisfying of your earnest request, as the performance of my promise made unto you at my last being with you in *England*, I have sent you (although in a homely style, especially for the contentation of a delicate ear) the true discourse of my last voyage into the West *Indies*, and parts of *America* called *Virginia*, taken in hand about the end of February, in the year of our redemption 1590.

And what events happened unto us in this our journey, you shall plainly perceive by the sequel of my discourse. [1]

There were at the time aforesaid three ships absolutely determined to go for the West *Indies*, at the special charges of M. *John Wattes* of *London* Merchant. [2]

[1] *These opening words confirm that this letter was included with John White's account of the 1590 voyage when delivered to Hakluyt three years after the event.*
[2] *This John Wattes could be Sir John Watts, who was master of the Clothworkers' Company in 1594 and knighted in 1603 before finally becoming Lord Mayor of London in 1606–7. He died in 1616 [Stow's Survey of London: volume 8: Shoreditch 5-14].*

But when they were fully furnished, and in readiness to make their departure, a general stay was commanded of all ships throughout *England*. Which so soon as I heard, I presently (as I thought it most requisite) acquainted Sir *Walter Ralegh* therewith, desiring him that as I had sundry time afore been chargeable and troublesome unto him, for the supplies and reliefs of the planters in *Virginia*: to likewise, that by his endeavour it would please him at that instant to procure licence for those three ships to proceed on with their determined voyage, that thereby the people in *Virginia* (if it were Gods pleasure) might speedily be comforted and relieved without further charges unto him.

Whereupon he by his good means obtained licence of the Queens majesty, and orders to be taken, that the owner of the 3 ships should be bound unto Sir *Walter Ralegh* or his assigns, in 3000 pounds, that those 3 ships in consideration of their releasement should take in, and transport a convenient number of passengers, with their furnitures and necessaries to be landed in *Virginia*.

Nevertheless that order was not observed, neither was the bond taken according to the intention aforesaid. But rather in contempt of the aforesaid order, I was by the owner and Commanders of the ships denied to have any passengers, or any thing else transported in any of the said ships, saving only myself and my chest; no not so much as a boy to attend upon me, although I made great suit, and earnest entreaty as well to the chief Commanders, as to the owner of the said ships. Which cross and unkind dealing, although it very much discontented me, not withstanding the scarcity of time was such that I could have no opportunity to go unto Sir *Walter Ralegh* with complaint: for the ships being then all in readiness to go to the Sea, would have been departed before I could have made my return.

Thus both Governors, Masters, and sailors, regarding very smally the good of their countrymen in Virginia; determined nothing less than to touch at those places, but wholly disposed themselves to seek after purchase and spoils, spending so much time therein, that Summer was spent before we arrived at *Virginia*.

And when we were come thither, the season was so unfit, and weather so foul, that we were constrained of force to forsake that coast, having not seen any of our planters, with loss on one of our ship-boats, and 7 of our chiefest men: and also with loss of 3 of our anchors and cables, and most of our casks with the fresh water left on shore, not possible to be had aboard.

Which evils and unfortunate events (as well to their own loss as to the hindrance of the planters in *Virginia*) had not chanced, if the order set down by Sir *Walter Ralegh* had been observed, or if my daily and continual petitions for the performance of the same might have taken any place.

Thus may you plainly perceive the success of my fifth and last voyage to *Virginia*, which was no less unfortunately ended then forwardly begun, and as luckless to many, as sinister to myself.

But I would to God it had been as prosperous to all, as noisome to the planters; and as joyful to me, as discomfortable to them.

Yet seeing it is not my first crossed voyage, I remain contented. And wanting my wishes, I leave off from prosecuting that whereunto I would to God my wealth were answerable to my will.

Thus committing the relief of my discomfortable company the planters in Virginia, to the merciful help of the Almighty, whom I most humbly beseech to help and comfort them, according to his most holy will and their good desire, I take my leave from my house at *Newtowne* in *Kylmore* [3] the 4 of February, 1593.

Your most well-wishing friend
JOHN WHITE

[3] *'Newtowne in Kylmore' ~ This location is most likely Newtown near Kilmore Quay in County Wexford, Ireland, although some authorities place this Newtown to the west of Cork. Research in Ireland has not revealed the existence of John White's house, nor has any record been found of his death and subsequent burial.*

Female from the village of Aquascogoc

End of Transcriptions

Chapter Twelve

~

The Ships

I thought it fitting at this point to pay homage to the ships and captains of England, without whom none of this extraordinary saga would have taken place. What follows may be an incomplete list but it is the first attempt I know of to accurately record them.

* * *

1584 ~ Voyage of Amadas and Barlowe from Plymouth

The voyage was undertaken by two vessels described in Hakluyt's *Principal Navigations* (1589 version) as 'barks well furnished with men and victuals'. No other information has been uncovered about these ships.

* * *

1585 ~ Grenville's voyage with the military colony from Plymouth

Dorothy ~ 'a small bark'
Described as a pinnace in later accounts, this ship was

owned by Raleigh; details of her captain remain unknown.
Elizabeth ~ '50 tunnes'
Her captain was Thomas Cavendish.
Red Lyon ~ 'a hundred tunnes or thereabouts'
Her captain was George Raymond.
Roebuck ~ also written *Roe Buck*
She was described as a flyboat of about '140 tunnes' and
was owned by Grenville. Her captain was John Clarke.
Tyger ~ a ship of 'seven score tunne'
The *Tyger* was the admiral of the fleet, according to
Hakluyt. She was commanded and owned by Grenville,
with Simon Fernandez as chief pilot and master. This was
possibly a Spanish prize originally built around 1540 as a
galleass, an intermediate design between a rowed galley
and a true man-of-war typical of the late Elizabethan
period. She was probably rebuilt around 1570. She later
fought against the Spanish Armada in 1588, eventually
serving Grenville for possibly up to twenty years.

Also involved in this voyage were two unnamed
pinnaces of '20 to 30 tunnes' each. Hakluyt records that
they were intended 'for speedie services'. One was lost on
the outbound leg off Portugal. The loss was evidently a
strategic one for Grenville's party built its replacement at
Puerto Rico.

Prizes from the voyage:

Santa Maria de Vincente ~ of some '300 tunnes'
When in Spanish hands she was commanded by Captain
Alonzo Cornieles. This prize was later converted at
Bideford, and renamed the *Dudley*. Ironically, she took part

in the fight against the Spanish Armada in 1588, then under the captaincy of James Erisey.

'A large frigate' ~ (unnamed)
Originally owned by Lorenzo de Vallejo.

'A small frigate' ~ (unnamed)
Her captain was Don Fernando de Altamirano. This ship was used by Ralph Lane to carry salt dug at Cabo Rojo, Puerto Rico, on the way to Roanoke.

* * *

1586 ~ the main ships in Sir Francis Drake's fleet that evacuated Ralph Lane's colony from Roanoke.

Aide ~ 200-250 tons
She was the Queen's ship, her captain was Edward Winter. This ship fought against the Spanish Armada in 1588 under Captain William Fenner.

Bark Bond ~ 120-150 tons
Owned at least in part by John Hawkins, treasurer of the navy, and captained by Robert Crosse, she was another ship that also fought against the Spanish Armada in 1588, this time under Captain William Poole.

Bark Bonner ~ about 150 tons (inaccurately quoted as being '400 tunnes' in Hakluyt 1589)
Owned by William Hawkins and captained by George Fortescue, this is the vessel that Drake offered Lane after a

storm had scattered much of the fleet. She also fought against the Spanish Armada in 1588 under Captain Charles Coffin.

Benjamin ~
Her captain was John Martin.

Drake ~
Her captain was John Vaughan.

Ducke ~ 'a Galliot'
Her captain was Richard Hawkins.

Elizabeth Bonaventure ~ 600 tons
A colossal ship of the line owned by Queen Elizabeth. She was Sir Francis Drake's flagship, captained by Master Thomas Venner. This ship fought against the Spanish Armada in 1588 under the captaincy of the Earl of Cumberland.

Francis ~ 70 tons
She was owned by Drake and was under the command of Captain Thomas Moone. Drake offered her to Lane, but she was driven out to sea by the storm.

George ~
Her captain was John Varney.

Hope ~ 200 tons
Her captain was Edward Carlisle. She was another ship that fought against the Spanish Armada in 1588, under the

captaincy of John Rivers, who incidentally captained the *Vantage* on this voyage.

Leicester ~ 400 tons
She was a galleon captained by Rear Admiral Francis Knollys and also fought against the Spanish Armada in 1588 under Captain George Fenner, possibly a relative of the captain of the *Aide*.

Minion of Plymouth ~
Her captain was Thomas Seeley and her master was John Newsome.

Primrose ~ 300 tons
She was at least partly owned by John Hawkins and captained by Vice Admiral Martin Frobisher. Her journal, written by Thomas Cate, is an important source of information about Drake's West Indian voyage (see Chapter Five).

Sea Dragon ~ 140 tons
She was owned by Sir William Winter, the Queen's surveyor of ships. Her captain was Henry White. She was one of the vessels scattered by the storm that arose while the fleet rode at anchor off the Outer Banks. On her return, she needed new anchors and cables.

Scout ~
Her captain was Edward Gilman.

Swallow ~
Her captain was Bitfield.

Talbot ~ 'a bark of 150-200 tunnes'
She was owned by George Talbot, Earl of Shrewsbury, and captained by someone we know only as Bailie. No supporting evidence can be found to prove whether or not this was Roger Bailey, the assistant to John White, governor of the Lost Colony. Interestingly, she fought against the Spanish Armada in 1588 under a Captain Henry White; whether the White surname connection was purely coincidental cannot be ascertained.

Thomas ~ 100-200 tons
She was owned by Sir Francis Drake and her captain was his brother, Thomas Drake. She fought against the Spanish Armada under Captain Henry Spendlove. Whether Henry was related to the 'lost' colonist John Spendlove cannot be ascertained.

Tiger ~ 200 tons
Commanded by master and lieutenant general Christopher Carleill, this was Queen Elizabeth's ship and not Grenville's *Tyger* of 1585. This ship later fought against the Spanish Armada under Captain John Bostock.

Vantage ~
Her captain was John Rivers.

White Lion ~ 140-150 tons
This ship was a private man-of-war owned by Charles, Lord Howard of Effingham, Lord Admiral of England. Her captain was James Erisay, who went on to captain the *Dudley* in the fight against the Spanish Armada. The *White*

Lion also fought against the Spanish Armada under the captaincy of her owner Charles, Lord Howard. She lost an anchor and cable off the Outer Banks during Drake's attempt to render assistance to the Lane colony. It was Lord Howard who fled the island of Flores, leaving Grenville to his fate.

* * *

1586 ~ The relief voyages for the military colony

Name unknown ~ a supply ship of '100 tunnes'
She was owned and sent to Roanoke by Raleigh. She arrived after 19 June 1586, found Lane's settlement deserted, and soon left. No other details are known.

Roebuck and *Tyger* ~
Both ships had previously taken part in the 1585 voyage. They sailed from Bideford with four other unnamed ships and four hundred men shortly after the departure of Raleigh's ship, commanded by Sir Richard Grenville. Grenville arrived shortly after Raleigh's supply ship had departed.

Prizes:

Brave Peter ~
Later renamed the *Brave* and used in White's attempt of 1588, this ship was originally captured off Finisterre and sent home to Bideford on the outbound part of that voyage.

Julian of St. Brieuc ~
Captained by Master Peter Godbecin, she was also sent home to Bideford after capture off Finisterre on the outbound voyage. No record can be found to confirm that she became the *Roe* of 1588, but it would seem likely that she is one and the same.

Martin Johnson of Amsterdam ~ a flyboat
Being a good 'sailer' she was re-rigged and retained for the voyage.

Name unknown ~
This was a ship taken in the Azores.

* * *

1587 ~ The voyage to settle the planters' colony (now known as the Lost Colony) from Portsmouth and Plymouth

Lyon ~ '120 tunnes'
The *Lyon* was the admiral of the fleet, captained by Governor John White with Simon Fernandino as master.

An unidentified flyboat ~
Her master was Edward Spicer.

An unidentified pinnace ~
Her captain was Edward Stafford.

* * *

1588 ~ The first attempt to relieve the planters' colony; led by Sir Richard Grenville from Bideford

NB: Among the acts of the Privy Council for 1588 there is an order commandeering this fleet Grenville had prepared at Bideford for the relief of Roanoke, and directing them to Plymouth under his command, to take part in the impending fight against the Spanish Armada.

Dudley ~ 300 tons
This was the Spanish prize of 1585, captained by James Erisey, formerly captain of the *White Lion* in Drake's West Indies voyage of 1586.

Virgin God Save Her ~ 200 tons
This ship was captained by John Grenville, Grenville's second son, who died on Raleigh's voyage to Guyana in 1595.

Tyger ~ 140 tons
The *Tyger* was Grenville's flagship of 1585 and the flagship for this intended voyage.

Golden Hind ~ 50 tons
Described as a pinnace and captained by Thomas Fleming, this ship was the lookout ship tasked with spotting the approaching Spanish Armada. Renamed the *Bark Fleming,* allegedly at the request of Sir Francis Drake.

St Leger ~ 50 tons
This ship was described as a pinnace and captained by John St Leger's son (also known as John).

* * *

1588 ~ The second attempt to relieve the planters' colony; led by John White from Bideford

Brave ~ 30 tons
The *Brave* was described as a pinnace and commanded by Captain Arthur Facey of Bideford, with Pedro Diaz as pilot.

Roe ~ '25 tunnes'
This ship was commanded by Captain Philip Amadas.

* * *

1590 – The third attempt to relieve the planters' colony; led by John White, probably originally departing from London

Hopewell ~ 200 tons
The *Hopewell* was admiral of the fleet and captained by Abraham Cooke. Her master was Robert Hutton. This ship fought against the Spanish Armada under Captain John Marchant.

John Evangelist ~ a pinnace
Her captain was William Lane.

Little John ~ 120 tons
The *Little John* was vice admiral of the fleet and captained by Christopher Newport. Her master was Michael Geare.

Moonelight ~
Her captain was Edward Spicer.

Name unknown ~
This was a pinnace, possibly named *Conclude*. Her captain was Captain Harps.

Two unidentified shallops ~
These were lost under tow in the waters just off Plymouth.

Two 'Ship-Boats' ~
These were obtained from two 'ships of London' loading sugar at Santa Cruz.

Prizes:

A 'Double Flyboat' ~ taken off the Canaries
Two Spanish frigates ~ one of '10 tunnes'
Buen Jesus ~ 300-350 tons, from Seville
Trinidad ~ 60 tons

Village elder of Pomeiooc

Chapter Thirteen

~

The Colonists

When Sir Walter Raleigh finally set out to colonise America, he had a clear idea of the type of people he was going to need. He gained this knowledge from the report made for him during the 1584 exploratory voyage by Amadas and Barlowe, and from Richard Hakluyt's *Discourse on Western Planting* (See Reference 5), a discussion document written only two years earlier, originally intended to provide a persuasive argument for English settlement in America. The report from Amadas and Barlowe is covered in an earlier chapter, but it is worth making some observations on Hakluyt's *Discourse* as it gives us a great deal of information on the necessary skills the colonists were thought to require in order to survive and prosper in the New World. A trawl through the list of skills or trades required reveals a desire for:

Millwrights, sawyers and carpenters 'for buildinges'
Blacksmiths
Salt makers
Brick and tile makers and layers

Lime makers (evidence of attempts to make lime from seashells has recently been found on Hatteras)

Thatchers

Barbers (surgeons)

Tailors, cooks, bakers, brewers, butchers, shoemakers, tanners, skinners and dyers

Fowlers

Sea fishers and freshwater fishers (fishermen)

And at a perhaps more fascinating level:

Sugar cane, vine and olive planters

Hunters 'skilfull to kill wilde beasts for vittell' and warreners 'to breede conies (rabbits) and to kill vermin'

'Mynerall men' (presumably miners, but it could also be inferred to mean mineralogists to determine any practical value of the area's rocks and minerals)

'Synkers of welles and finders of springes'

It was clear, too, that the possibility of having to defend the colony did not go unconsidered, for Hakluyt also advises the coloniser to take:

'Men experte in the arte of fortification',

'Capitaines of longe and of greate experience'

'Souldiers well trayned in Flanders to joyne with the younger'

Hakluyt also considered the ability to harvest America and dispatch goods back to England to be important capabilities of any colony. His *Discourse* includes a requirement for:

'Burners of asshes for the trade of sope asshes (Potash)'
'Joyners, to cutt oute the boordes into chests to be imbarqued for England'
'Tallow chandlers, to prepare the tallowe to be incasked for England'
Shipwrights 'in some number'
Oar makers and makers of cable and cordage

Having identified the skills they needed, Raleigh and Grenville set out to recruit their colonists. Traditionally, the roster of those they selected for the venture has always been recognised as that first presented by Richard Hakluyt in 1589. However, what few realise is that this list is NOT a definitive roll call of the 'lost' colonists. It is merely, in Hakluyt's own words, 'those who remained on Roanoke 1587'. This can be verified by observing that both John White and Simon Ferdinando, who appear on that list, were later recorded by Hakluyt himself as having returned to England the same year.

To this discrepancy, we should add a number of names that appear on Raleigh's assignment of 1589 as being 'late of London', yet who do not appear on Hakluyt's colony list. Furthermore, there is the omission of Edward Stafford, whom we must now consider as having also remained in Roanoke.

There is a need therefore to re-evaluate Hakluyt's roster. To achieve this, we need to see the documents from which he derived these names. However, there are no known surviving original notes or manuscripts. This situation exists because the Elizabethans, including Hakluyt, tended to discard the original documents they were working from when they transcribed names and events. Thus we have no way of conducting that re-evaluation from first-hand accounts and have only Hakluyt's work and Raleigh's 1589 assignment from which to draw up a roster of those 1587 'lost' colonists. The following list has therefore been compiled from these two documents, with additional observations for genealogical purposes. (NB. Those 'lost' are given in bold type.)

The Twelve Assistants to the 'Cittie of Ralegh'

Roger Bailie (a possible relative of Walter Bayly, who was named by Raleigh's assignment as an investor in the colony?)
Christopher Cooper
Ananias Dare
Dyonis Harvie
George Howe (murdered by the native Indians)
Roger Prat
John Sampson
Thomas Stevens

These eight are listed with two more who appear in the same 'late of London' context in Raleigh's assignment yet who do not appear on Hakluyt's roster:

Humfrey Dimmocke
John Nichols

Also of note in Raleigh's assignment is that George Howe is listed in a separate context, as being of the 'other part', i.e. of Virginia, with two others:

William Fulwood
James Plat

Since Raleigh would have known of George Howe's murder at the time the assignment was drawn up, we have to consider that William Fulwood and James Plat may have also been assistants who were deceased at the time it was drawn up, perhaps, in their case, dying during the voyage to Virginia.

The Families

Arnold Archard, **Joyce Archard** and their son **Thomas Archard**
Ananias Dare (already listed above) and **Elyoner Dare** (née White) and their daughter **Virginia Dare**
Dyonis Harvie (already listed above) and **Margery Harvie** and their **unnamed son**
Ambrose Viccars, **Elizabeth Viccars** and their son **Ambrose Viccars**

The (Likely) Married Couples

John Chapman and **Alis Chapman**
Thomas Colman and **Joan Colman** (Mrs Colman's Christian name is not given but there is one marriage record of the period which suggests she could have been Joan Coleman née Rudd)
John Jones and **Jane Jones**
Edward Powell and **Wenefrid Powell**
Henry Payne and **Rose Payne**

Thomas Topan and **Audry Tappan** (are these two subject to a possible spelling mistake? Research cannot find a marriage record of the Topan surname so they may not be husband and wife, but in the Elizabethan period spellings were often phonetically based and therefore subject to personal interpretation)

Thomas Warner and **Joan Warren** (is this also a possible spelling mistake? There is a marriage record of a Joan Barnes to a Thomas Warner from which there are no children recorded)

The (Likely) Fathers and Sons

Thomas Ellis and **Robert Ellis**
George Howe (already listed above) and **George Howe**
Roger Prat (already listed above) and **John Prat**
John Sampson (already listed above) and **John Sampson**

The Single Women
(perhaps betrothed? We simply do not know)

Elizabeth Glane (possible spelling error? There is no trace of this surname in any known archive)
Margaret Lawrence
Jane Mannering
Emme Merrimoth (possible spelling error? There is no trace of this surname in any known archive)
Jane Pierce
Agnes Wood

The (Likely) Orphans

Thomas Humfrey
Tomas Smart
William Wythers

The Single Men
(presumed not to have left a spouse back in England)

Morris Allen
Richard Arthur
Marke Bennet
William Berde
Henry Berrye
Richard Berrye
Michael Bishop
John Borden
John Bridger
John Bright
John Brooke
Henry Browne
William Browne
John Burden
Thomas Butler
Anthony Cage
John Cheven
William Clement
John Cotsmur (possible surname spelling error? A modern equivalent has not been identified)
Richard Darige (possible surname spelling error; perhaps Davidge?)

Henry Dorrell
William Dutton
Edmond English
John Earnest
John Farre
Charles Florrie
John Gibbes
Thomas Gramme
Thomas Harris (possible relative of Gabriel Harris, who was named by Raleigh's assignment as an investor in the colony?)
Thomas Harris (a second man with that name)
John Hemmington (possible surname spelling error; perhaps Herrington?)
Thomas Hewet
James Hynde
Henry Johnson
Nicholas Johnson
Griffen Jones
Richard Kemme (possible surname spelling error; perhaps Kemis or Keynes?)
James Lasie
Peter Little
Robert Little
William Lucas
George Martyn (possible relative of Thomas Martin, who was named by Raleigh's assignment as an investor in the colony?)
Michael Myllet
Henry Mylton
Humfrey Newton

William Nicholes

Hugh Pattenson (possible surname spelling error; perhaps Patterson?)

Thomas Phevens (possible surname spelling error? A modern equivalent has not been identified)

Henry Rufoote (possible surname spelling error? A modern equivalent has not been identified)

Thomas Scot

Richard Shaberdge (possible surname spelling error? A modern equivalent has not been identified)

Thomas Smith (possible relative of Thomas Smith, named by Raleigh's assignment as an investor in the colony?)

William Sole

John Spendlove

Edward Stafford (captain of the pinnace that remained at Roanoke)

John Starte

John Stilman

Martyn Sutton

Clement Tayler

Richard Taverner

Hugh Tayler

Richard Tomkins

John Tydway (possible surname spelling error; perhaps Tideway?)

William Waters

Cutbert White

Richard Wildye

Robert Wilkinson

William Willes

Lewes Wotton
John Wright (possible relative of Richard Wright, named by Raleigh's assignment as an investor in the colony?)
Brian Wyles
John Wyles

The high number of single men may have resulted from some of them, perhaps up to twenty-five or so, being crew members of the pinnace. The concept of these men being crewmen or mariners is not so far-fetched as it might seem. If we go back a moment to Hakluyt's *Discourse*, we will find that it contains a clear instruction that the colony should have 'pinesses with experte Seamen'. It is therefore highly improbable that the colony would have been left an empty pinnace without an experienced crew to sail her.

Finally, given these revisions to the roster of colonists, the number 'lost' (other than the unnamed thirteen or possibly sixteen from Grenville's 1586 voyage) should now stand at **119**.

A Campfire Ceremony

Chapter Fourteen

~

Questions, Answers; Answers, Questions

Before analyzing the attempt by Sir Water Raleigh to settle a colony in what is now North Carolina, we must first accept that whilst the events of that extraordinary seven-year period in Elizabethan history read like some Boy's Own book, they are so well documented by first-hand accounts, the efforts of Hakluyt, and through the support of numerous fragments from various State Papers and private records both here and in Spain, the latter of which could not have been known to Hakluyt at the time of his narrations, that there cannot be, and should not be, any doubt regarding the story's authenticity.

And what a story it is: two ill-fated colonies and no less than eight voyages, successful and unsuccessful, in just seven years. Yet for all this, it is truly a story of 'If only's'. To say the failure to settle Roanoke successfully between 1584 and 1590 was due to a series of unfortunate events might be a considerable understatement.

If only, for example, Ralph Lane had not decided to take the opportunity to return to England with Sir Francis Drake; but then, if only Sir Francis Drake, ever the one to meddle in Grenville's and Raleigh's plans, had not decided to call in on their colony on his way back from plundering the Spanish West Indies. If only Raleigh's unnamed ship sent in 1586 had arrived a few days earlier or Grenville's ships of the same year had arrived a couple of weeks earlier. If only Grenville's fifteen men had done as they undoubtedly had been told to do, and remained defensive of the English foothold in Virginia, even if that meant living with the known-to-be friendly Croatoan Indians. If only Simon Ferdinando had done as he was told to do and had left the planters' colony at Chesapeake Bay. If only the foolhardy captain of the *Brave* in 1588 had not engaged in futile warfare with every ship he could find, all invariably so much larger than his; and from the same voyage, if only Captain Amadas onboard the *Roe* had carried on with the mission rather than simply giving up and returning to England. One could even argue that if only Mother Nature had been a little kinder to John White in 1590 or, for that matter, to Sir Francis Drake and Ralph Lane in 1585; but, of course, if only the Spanish Armada had not chosen to attack England in 1588, that might have changed the course of history, too!

Indeed if only just one scrap of fortune or timing had been a fraction better, we might not now be thinking of Jamestown or the efforts of the Plymouth Brethren as the first settlements in America, but instead, of Roanoke, or, as Sir Walter Raleigh called it (and which is now the title granted to Manteo, the picturesque town that resides on the site today) the 'Cittie of Ralegh'.

Nevertheless, for all the documentation that exists, there remains a whole raft of debates, not only about what happened to the planters' colony of 1587, but also about exactly which interpretations should be applied to the original accounts describing the whole series of events that took place during this period in English history. One of the great problems with this is the reliance of so many modern writers on the work of David Beers Quinn in his one-time authoritative book *Set Fair for Roanoke*, first published more than fifty years ago. That reliance has led to a plethora of hypothesizing, which, as time has passed by, appears to have become wilder and more fanciful; so much so that it could be argued it is difficult to unearth the original story. When I set out to conduct my own research, I did so with the clear intent of using as much original material as I could find, from which to form the theories and interpretations set out in this book.

Taking the events in chronological order therefore, let us first review the voyage of Amadas and Barlowe in 1584.

To start with, the landing place of their arrival is confused. Some authorities place this as being just north of what is now modern-day Buxton on Hatteras, through an inlet (known then as Chacandepeco). If we look at the account given of that landing we find that exactly where Amadas and Barlowe landed could be determined as Ocracoke (Wokocon) (as so noted in the margin of Hakluyt's 1600 edition of his work), Hatteras (Croatoan) for reasons stated above, or, as the author interprets, closer to Bodie Island some sixty miles north of Hatteras.

The argument for this last conclusion is:

1. Captain Barlowe, when identifying Roanoke, and referring to their ships, states that Roanoke was 'distant

from the harbour by which we entered, seven leagues', i.e. approximately twenty-one miles. The Ocracoke (Wococon) inlet was in excess of eighty miles distant and Chacandepeco at Hatteras around sixty. Only the Bodie Island area would therefore have been close enough.

2. Hatteras island was thought to have been a seasonal habitation, but recent surveys and archaeological examination of Hatteras, now make it clear the island was almost certainly subject to permanent occupation. Amadas and Barlowe, even with the most modest exploration, did not discover any village or note any signs of habitation. If they had indeed landed on Hatteras, surely they would have seen something? For example, we know the Croatoan people who lived on Hatteras burned the stubble from their crops. Widespread burning would have been seen and recognised as burned stubble by Amadas and Barlowe, as the practice was, until recently, commonplace back in England. The same argument appears reasonable for Ocracoke too. Bodie Island on the other hand was uninhabited.

3. Amadas and Barlowe's ships would have been highly visible. If Amadas and Barlowe had landed by an inhabited island, it makes no sense that it would take two days before the Indians showed themselves to the English, especially given that we now know the Indians were there in great numbers and were a curious and unafraid people.

4. Amadas and Barlowe fired a gun but no one came or responded. If this had been an inhabited island, the shot

would have been heard by the population. It seems impossible to believe therefore that the Indians would not have responded in some form to the unfamiliar and deafening sound of gunshot.

5. The Croatoans arrived in boats, not on land. If the anchorage had been at Hatteras or Ocracoke, surely the Indians, given that we now believe they were on the island, would have walked down the beach to Amadas and Barlowe rather than arrive by canoe? If the English had anchored near the uninhabited Bodie Island, then the Croatoan Indians arrival by boat would make much more sense.

The solution to the above debate would be to know precisely which inlet Amadas and Barlowe passed through. The author spent much time researching this issue and found that there have been numerous studies and maps made of the area. In the hope of finding some clues, this is what was unearthed:

Dirk Frankenburg's '*The Nature of the Outer Banks*' (See Reference 6) and David Stick's '*The Outer Banks of North Carolina 1584 – 1958*' (See Reference 7) state that before 1657 there were six openings to the sea. However, maps by Hessel Gerritsz (1630), Willem Jansz (1638), and Johannes Janssonius (1639) show only four: one either side of Bodie Island (Port Lane and Port Ferdinando); the original inlet at Hatteras (known as Old Hatteras), about three miles further south into Ocracoke than the inlet we see today; and one at Wokokon (between Ocracoke and Portsmouth Island, which has never closed in recorded history).

Theodor de Bry's map of circa 1600 also shows one of Frankenburg and Stick's inlets just south of the modern town of Duck, an inlet de Bry refers to as Trinity. It is an inlet that does not appear on White's original drawing, though, and Ralph Lane, when writing from Port Ferdinando on 12 August 1585, describes only three inlets in the coast, each of which he names. Importantly, his letter was written some time before he ventured north to the Currituck Sound and therefore he would probably not have known of the existence of de Bry's 'Trinity Harbour' at the time he wrote his letter. Thus we have to conclude that de Bry's Trinity may be a mistake.

The other inlet of Frankenburg and Stick, not mentioned in detail here, is one which both White and de Bry show at Chacandepeco, just north of modern-day Buxton. John White's map shows a 'wash' running at this inlet, suggesting perhaps that it may have been shallow or in the process of forming or closing in 1585. Ogilby-Moxon's map of circa 1672 shows it closed. When surveyor John Lawson visited the Hatteras area in 1701, he makes no mention of its existence in his analysis of the inlets along the Outer Banks region. Given the detail of the historical maps and notes quoted here, therefore, we may have to consider that this inlet was (and perhaps remains) unstable.

If we accept that there may have been four inlets open in 1584, and that Amadas and Barlowe had landed in an uninhabited area, then given that two of the inlets are near habitation, they can only have landed near Bodie Island.

N.B. In examining references to these inlets, the map reputedly drawn by Velasco in 1611 showing remarkable detail of the Outer Banks was ignored on the basis that it is considered a forgery (David Y. Allen, map librarian at Stony Brook University in New York).

When Amadas and Barlowe finally made contact with the Indians, what must have alarmed them most were the stories of at least two previous encounters with 'white men'. There are, to date, no known accounts of English or French ships foundering in these waters, so given their proximity to Florida it seems logical that these mariners had to be Spanish, a thought that must have crossed the minds of Amadas and Barlowe. It therefore seems odd that they made no attempt to establish more about these mariners or locate any remnant of their ships. We can only assume that they took at face value the Indians' story that none survived to tell whoever their masters were of the existence of the Outer Banks and its Indians, and thus they were considered to pose no threat to the expected English settlements.

Amadas and Barlowe returned home to England with rather inflated stories of a bountiful land, enough for Raleigh to finance the next step in his colonisation attempts. Due to the attentions of Queen Elizabeth, however, Raleigh had to defer charge of these attempts to his cousin, Sir Richard Grenville. Thus, 1585 dawned with Grenville's extraordinary voyage and the detailed accounts of Lane's ill-fated stay on Roanoke. These accounts not only give us a great deal of commentary on Grenville and his character but also significant information on the forts, explorations and discoveries of Ralph Lane. There appears to have been little recognition heretofore of the value of what these accounts tell us.

First, they contain Lane's designs for the fortresses he built, which ultimately are probably the most physical evidence we have by which to search archaeologically for the colonists. We know Lane preferred to build his forts close by the water's edge to use the sea as an effective barrier and additional access point. We can support this theory by observing that from the description of the surrounding geography, Ralph Lane's fort on or by Tallaboa Bay on St John (Puerto Rico), for example, was by the sea. From Pedro Diaz's deposition, it appears that the location of the Roanoke fort was also near the water's edge.

The accounts also give us a strong suggestion of the probable layout of any fort Lane built. We know he built them at Port Ferdinando (or Bodie Island), on Roanoke, and, most intriguingly, somewhere on the James River, a point that appears not to have been recognised by some historians. Lane had a liking for building triangular forts, a practice still in evidence at the Jamestown settlement twenty years later. It is only in the plainly elaborate fort at Cabo Rojo, built while taking salt, that Lane appears to deviate from his preferred design. Thus when searching for the remains of any of Lane's forts one should expect to find them all roughly triangular in form and close to the water's edge, yet sadly so far none have been formally identified.

Elsewhere in the account of Grenville's voyage there is the fascinating story of their stay on St John (now Puerto Rico), and in particular of the meeting under a flag of truce between the English and Spanish soldiers. In it, Grenville claims that he sent his men out to meet the Spanish to tell them that they were merely replenishing supplies and making repairs, signalling that they did not seek any trouble with the Spanish. Yet, from the Spanish archives, we get a slightly different picture. Their version confirms what Grenville claimed but adds that the English had declared they were in possession of Spanish hostages they were intending to ransom in New Spain (Florida). Either this was an excuse made up by the Spanish commander to suggest that he did not want to risk the lives of his countrymen, thus avoiding facing awkward questions as to why he did not attack the fort, or it was a bluff by Grenville to deter the Spanish from attacking. Who was right, we can only guess.

There followed a landing at Roxo Bay (Cabo Rojo, Puerto Rico) where Ralph Lane showed his quality of bravado when he had twenty of his men surround a salt hill on the beach and dig in for an expected skirmish with the Spanish. Salt was a valuable commodity and essential for the existence of both the Spanish and the English colonies. What followed with the arrival of the Spanish forces can only be described as a tense stand-off as the Spaniards watched Lane's men literally steal the valuable salt in front of their eyes, while the men of both sides waited and watched, probably only a few yards apart, for the order to attack and face certain bloodshed and possible death.

We come then to the great feast of Hispaniola, taking place as it did at a time when relations between England and Spain were rapidly declining. In boldly coming ashore, was it Grenville's plan to intimidate the Spanish into thinking the English he commanded were so powerful as to be able to act with an almost belligerent impunity? Or did the Spanish simply take Grenville's offer of a feast as an opportunity to break the monotony of their existence? We may never know.

What the author believes is that the event took place simply because the Spanish governor considered himself a man of Grenville's equal. Hence the reason why the Spaniards, in complement to Grenville's feast, offered what must have been a magnificent sporting sight as both sides' finest rode side by side, hunting down their quarry along the shoreline.

Again, though, both the English and Spanish accounts differ slightly in what Grenville wanted from the visit. The English account states that Grenville intended to barter for horses, cattle and victuals, whereas the Spanish account states that he 'demanded' these. Either way, he obviously got what he came for. Perhaps, however, the most revealing note from this encounter is the Spanish observations of the 'English' Indians (Manteo and Wanchese) who are described as speaking English, having a great love of music, and being 'richly dressed'. This is the only known description we have of them.

The journey to Roanoke was not without other dangers, too. The record of the voyage includes a description wherein the fleet was anchored at an island in order to take seals (for food). In attempting to do so, Grenville and several others 'were in very great danger to have been cast away', although the reason why is not revealed.

Then of course we read that the *Tyger*, Grenville's flagship and no doubt his pride and joy for it appears several times in his life history, ran aground at the entrance to the inlet between Ocracoke and Hatteras (Croatoan) and was badly damaged. It is very likely the ship was carrying some of the livestock that Grenville acquired from Hispaniola, being one of the few large enough to hold this cargo; we know it was carrying a considerable amount of 'victuals' for the military colony, too. Given that the damage was obviously significant enough for the ship to be repaired where she foundered, it is certain the ship was emptied of its cargo in situ while the repairs took place. An intrigue from the consequences of this is that Grenville could be responsible for one of Ocracoke Island's great mysteries.

The island today has a dwindling population of Spanish horses and no one knows where they came from or indeed when they arrived. There are two principal theories: one, that Lucas Vazquez de Ayllon's failed colony of 1526, established near the Santee River in South Carolina, abandoned them when the colony left; and two, that they are indeed the horses left behind by Grenville, probably escaping when his ship ran aground on the island. Grenville has to be the obvious choice for the reason that any horses left behind by de Ayllon's colony would have had to travel many miles northward along the coast and negotiate at least three open sea inlets to arrive on Ocracoke, while the grounding of Grenville's ship merely required them to perhaps splash ashore. There is also the rather enlightening, if tangential, possibility that the term 'Banker' horse, the description by which they are known today, could be a corruption of 'Barter' horse. Grenville, after all, bartered for his horses at Hispaniola.

One popular misconception we must dispel in the Grenville and Lane accounts of 1585 is the incident involving the theft of a silver cup. Some authorities state that in reprisal for the theft, the native Indians were 'sled' or 'slayed'. The simple truth is they had not been 'sled' but had in fact 'fled' from the village. Given the vagaries of Elizabethan secretarial handwriting script it is not surprising that this mistake has often been made; the letter 's' of this handwriting form is regularly mistaken for an 'f'. We must realise, too, that skirmishes were a way of life among the Indians, thus they were well rehearsed at evacuation when attacked. It is therefore unthinkable that they would have stayed and watched the slaughter of their own. It is also unlikely that Lane, a man who displayed compassion on several occasions, would have seen genocide as an appropriate punishment for the probably lost silver cup.

When Grenville finally left Lane's colony on Roanoke later that same eventful year and proceeded home, luck was with him, for he came upon a Spanish ship lying at Bermuda. How he took that ship, though, is recorded as only Hollywood could write the words: 'boarding her with a boat made with boards of chests, which fell asunder, and sunk at the ships side, as soon as ever he and his men were out of it' (see page 61).

This does take some believing, for Grenville, having sighted the ship twice his size, must have ordered his amazed crew to lash some sea chests together into a makeshift raft and throw it over the side. They then rowed it across to the Spanish ship with Grenville either seated or standing at the fore of the raft, all the time being watched in utter disbelief by the Spanish crew and captain as he approached the ship. Disbelief must be the right word, for it would have been a simple task to blow him out of the water or kill him with a well-aimed bullet.

It was aboard this Spanish ship that Grenville captured a Portuguese pilot, one Pedro Diaz. The consequences of this action could hardly have been more fortuitous for the historian, for Diaz was held captive by Grenville for four years. During this time he visited Roanoke at least once before finally escaping from Grenville's clutches while ironically aboard a later voyage to Roanoke that was attacked by the French. (This was John White's ill-fated voyage of 1588.)

As an aside, later, in 1589, when Diaz made his deposition to the Spanish authorities in Havana recalling his extraordinary adventure, he spoke not only about Grenville's voyage home of 1585 but also the voyage of 1586 and his time as a prisoner of Grenville (along with approximately twenty Spaniards). The most fascinating comment of which is his account of being made to help build Grenville's house at Bideford. It is extraordinary to consider the thought of Spanish slaves working on projects in the rural tranquillity of small-town England, not to mention the question of where they may be buried today.

Let us return now, though, to Ralph Lane and his military colony back at Roanoke. We know from his account that he spent a great deal of time building perhaps more than one fort and we also know that he travelled some considerable distances in exploration of the surrounding region, quoting 130 miles on at least two occasions. Even allowing for some inaccuracies, there is evidence in his accounts that gives us clues to the areas he reached. These make for significant reading. For example, from his own description of the voyage north, he records the existence of a barren channel also running north. It appears that what Lane is describing is now known as the Currituck Sound. Given a short overland crossing at its furthest reaches, Lane could have reached Chesapeake Bay and the James River by this route if his measurement was even only vaguely accurate.

Once on the James River, Lane talks of raising a fort there, and this prospect raises intriguing questions:

1. When John Smith chose the James River for his site at Jamestown in 1607, was Lane's account of some twenty-two years past used as a guide to locate that site?

2. Since it is conceivable that the fort built by Lane in the James River area would most likely have been identical in its triangular design to that currently being described as the original Jamestown 1607 fort, was that later fort built over Lane's original? And if this is not the case, does this mean that Lane's fort is still awaiting discovery elsewhere in the James River?

The other great journey Lane made was to find the source of what he thought was some type of gold, to be found at the fabled location of Chaunis Temoatan, a location he seems to have been very close to finding judging by the Indian reception he got. Nevertheless, the author of this book is certain that given the detailed account of how the Indians extracted the metal, it was neither gold nor copper, but iron pyrite or fool's gold. Technically, copper and gold have similar melting points of around 2000 degrees Fahrenheit (1100 degrees centigrade), while iron pyrite melts at 850 degrees Fahrenheit (or 450 degrees centigrade), less than half the temperature of copper or gold. Even accounting for deep reservations over the description of how the 'copper' presented itself in the ore the Indians used, it is not unrealistic to consider that if indeed it was copper or gold, reaching the required temperatures to extract it would not have been an easy task for the native Indians to achieve, especially given that all they used was an open wood fire. It is of interest to note that the source of the Nottoway River, which Lane was probably traversing, is in the centre of the Virginian gold/pyrite ridge.

One of the most intriguing aspects of the Grenville voyage of 1585, though, is just what his relationship was like with Ralph Lane. To answer this we must turn to the one singular letter that mentions their relationship, which Lane prepared on September 8th for Walsingham. The letter gives us the now famous description of Grenville as showing 'intolerable pride, insatiable ambition, and proceedings towards them all, and to Lane in particular'. Given that at the time Lane wrote it, Grenville had already been gone more than a week and Lane had no way of knowing when he would be able to deliver it, it seems extraordinary that he held on to it for almost a year before the untimely arrival of Drake finally allowed him to deliver it.

The description of Grenville's character in that letter is probably not untypical but it is worth exploring the motive Lane must have had in order to write that letter and then retain it, still to stand by its contents so much later. The truth is that Lane was in a bitter legal dispute with Grenville and had been so for some time. There can be no doubt that sharing one's life with one's antagonist for several months in the confines of ships at sea and in the confines of a small settlement in a foreign land must have made for an interesting battle of wills. Nevertheless, neither Lane nor Grenville mentions this dispute, or any arguments that may have taken place, in their accounts of the voyage, or subsequently.

Perhaps the most significant legacy of Lane's occupation of Roanoke is the fort he built there that was the military colony's principal place of occupation throughout their stay. The National Park Service of America has proclaimed for many years that the earthworks apparent at the northeast tip of Roanoke are the remains of Lane's fort. However, it is perhaps rather embarrassing to report that these earthworks are most certainly not Lane's fort, but were probably built during the American Civil War. This is supported by archaeological evidence that, while confirming that Lane's men were almost certainly in the area, uncovered finds from beneath the earth banks of the fort that prove the banks were raised much later. The Park Service earthworks are therefore perhaps more correctly labelled 'Paine's Fort' after the commander who most likely built them nearly three hundred years after Lane left.

One facet of Lane's fort on Roanoke is that on rereading the Hakluyt texts, it is clear that Lane's officers lived separately from the men. Are we now also looking for a second fort? Or did they perhaps live with the Indians in the nearby village? It is yet another question left unanswered.

Perhaps the greatest question many historians ask of the military colony, though, is why Lane chose to abandon Roanoke when offered a lift home by Drake. In his account he pleads a great deal about the sorry state of his men, but evidently Drake had brought in some supplies by the time the decision was made to abandon the place, irrespective of how difficult that process proved to be. While the condition of his men must have played on the benevolent mind of Lane, he does give away another reason in his account: his clear intent to have abandoned Roanoke in 'but three months time regardless'. Why therefore prolong the inevitable?

Yet, had he waited just two weeks more, Grenville would have showed up with ample supply, let alone the single and still unidentified ship that Raleigh had sent over a few days earlier. The crew of Raleigh's ship must almost have had sight of Drake's fleet disappearing over the horizon back towards England complete with Lane's entire company, such was its almost immediate arrival.

We close this episode, though, with another fortuitous eyewitness account, that of Thomas Cate, who was on board Drake's relieving fleet. It contains much confirmation of Lane's account surrounding the relief of the military colony, but with one notable difference. Cate records that Lane left with 103 men, four fewer than the list Hakluyt prepared of those whom Grenville left with Lane the previous year. Lane states that all his men were accounted for yet clearly there is a discrepancy. Many theorists suggest these four may simply have been left behind, for we know that Lane scattered his men to at least three other locations in the hope of finding food. This is not the case. The answer comes from the deposition of Pedro Diaz four years later, in which he states that they had died, and from the account of Grenville in 1586, which confirms the discovery of at least one body.

So now we come to the 1586 voyages. Raleigh's ship remains a mystery. With none of the more learned scholars of past years having discovered its origins, there seems little chance of ever finding out her name, the name of the man who captained her, or indeed the location of the port from where she set sail.

Grenville's voyage from Bideford, however, is better known, but it is still only generically covered by Hakluyt. It is from the invaluable deposition of Pedro Diaz that we learn more. To begin with, Grenville, on arrival back after the 1585 expedition, must have started immediately on planning his return at Raleigh's request, and within a matter of a few months he set off again for Roanoke. He would not have had the wildest idea that Drake had decided to call in on an apparent whim to check out how Lane's military colony was faring; nor of course would he have known that Lane was to accept Drake's offer of a lift home. Instead, Grenville arrived fully expecting to be greeted by Lane, yet found Roanoke deserted, with little or no clue as to where they had gone save for the probable existence of a handful of scattered belongings and military paraphernalia.

There is no account of Grenville's time on Roanoke, although it is clear he did spend time searching for Lane's colony, and there is a strong suggestion he may have even met with the Croatoan Indians. If he did, then he would have probably established that Drake had relieved them barely two weeks prior to his arrival.

In any event Grenville obviously then plotted to leave a small garrison of fifteen men (eighteen in Diaz's account) in charge of Queen Elizabeth's new possession of Virginia, an area already perceived to have been many times that of the United Kingdom, whilst he returned to England for yet more men and supplies.

One fascinating legacy from the 1586 voyage is the resolution of one of England's great untold mysteries, that of 'Rawley a Winganditoian', the mysterious entry that appears in the parish register of St Mary's Church, Bideford. Rawley was, according to Diaz's account, one of three native Indians captured during a skirmish Grenville had while looking for Lane's colony. Two are recorded as escaping. The one that remained was brought back to England, baptised and finally laid to rest in Bideford's parish churchyard as the first Native American buried on English soil.

When Grenville finally returned to England, we should have little doubt that the words exchanged between him and Lane, perhaps in the presence of Raleigh, must have been positively hostile. It is for this fool's venture, Grenville would have thought, that he had sailed over four hundred leagues (according to Diaz), not only in attempting the resupply of the Roanoke colony but also, because of sickness on board his ships, crossing and re-crossing the Atlantic in search of a place of respite for his sick men and for a prize by which to make the voyage profitable.

As an aside, when Grenville finally found that prize, it was little more than a passenger ship, on which he evidently acted in the manner of a man who had been simmering with rage for many weeks. His actions, as a result, were disappointingly little more than those of a common pirate. It was from this ship that Grenville obtained additional slave labour to build his house on Bideford quay.

Grenville's attempts to hold Virginia also proved to be

in vain, for by the time the 1587 planters' colony arrived, his fifteen men had disappeared without a trace. What we learn of their fate comes only from the Indians who told John White in 1587 that at least two were killed and the remainder moved to the fort at Hatorask (Bodie Island), from where they simply vanished.

What happened to those men is conjectural. There are no records as yet discovered of any Englishmen being captured by the French or Spanish, and they would not have known of Lane's plans to relocate to Chesapeake Bay, making it unlikely they would have tried to reach that area. Thus, either there are the bodies of thirteen (or possibly sixteen Englishmen if Diaz is correct), lying undiscovered somewhere on the Outer Banks of North Carolina, or they have became at least partly responsible for the catalogue of mysterious sightings of Indians with European traits that now permeate the early history of English settlements in America.

The year 1587 dawned with Grenville in London organising a colony of planters for Roanoke. Diaz states that he was looking for a total of 210 people. He got barely half that number, and it seems increasingly certain that they were not all from London. Indeed it is conceivable that few of them had origins from that city.

Wherever they came from, a departure by ship from London is not recorded; all we have is a departure from Portsmouth. The departure from Portsmouth raises yet more questions though, for we know from the accounts that the ships sailed for barely an hour across the Solent to anchor at Cowes on the Isle of Wight, where they spent no less than eight days. It could be argued that this stay was purely for want of a favourable wind, but then surely the busy port of Portsmouth would have had an adequate network of ship's captains coming and going by which to obtain well-informed reports of sea conditions? Such a resource should have enabled White and Ferdinando to set a more favourable departure date, and negate the risk of wasting valuable onboard supplies while languishing in the Solent.

There is, however, an alternative theory as to why the ships stayed over at Cowes. The Carews, a West Country family who owned Carisbrooke Castle near Newport on the Isle of Wight and who were certainly resident there at the time, were well known to Raleigh and Grenville. It is not a giant leap to consider that some of those on board the ships simply stopped off for a social call and to ask the Carews if they could add to the number of colonists already in transit.

It is even conceivable that John White was perhaps formally instructed by Raleigh to visit Carisbrooke to ask the Carews if they could spare some of their workforce to make up the currently less-than-desired number of colonists Raleigh and Grenville had recruited. We may never know, but it is difficult to believe that White and perhaps some of his administrators spent an entire eight days on board, riding at anchor within swimming distance of time ashore, and never made that journey. Some days later the fleet arrived at Plymouth, where they stayed for a further two days, no doubt to top up supplies but perhaps also to take on yet more colonists.

Later, after much pottering around the West Indies, Captain Simon Ferdinando (sometimes written 'Fernando') finally obeyed his instructions from Raleigh and headed for the Chesapeake Bay, the place first recommended by Amadas and Barlowe three years earlier as being the most suitable for colonial settlement. Yet he never made it there. Ferdinando clearly had other ideas and, feigning a lack of time to get to the Chesapeake, he simply dumped the entire colony on Roanoke. When they arrived there, of course, they probably expected to be greeted by Grenville's fifteen men stationed on Roanoke only the previous year, but as with so much of the mystery of Roanoke, there was no sign of them.

Many words have been written on the colony of 1587, the so-called Lost Colony, so there is little one can add. Yet there are a couple of points worth noting. The first, quite extraordinary point, and one which is something of a revelation, is that the transcription of the names of the 1587 colony in Hakluyt's 1589 volumes includes Captain Simon Ferdinando, yet at the conclusion of the same account, Hakluyt declares that Ferdinando arrived back at Portsmouth.

On closer scrutiny of Hakluyt's narrative, one realises that it is in fact Captain Edward Stafford who remained at Roanoke and what is more, he did so with a pinnace, a ship more than capable of ferrying the entire colony the relatively short distance to the Chesapeake Bay or for that matter southward to Croatoan (Hatteras). Given that Stafford's ship had also readily made it across the Atlantic, it was obviously therefore also capable of making its own relief voyage to England. What happened to that pinnace remains a great mystery, but we can be certain that its discovery could provide a major clue as to what happened to the 'lost' colonists.

The second aspect of the 1587 voyage, and one that most historians question, is just why did the colonists persist so intently in their wish to make John White return to England, and just why did he finally decide to do so alone, especially given that his daughter and granddaughter were to remain on Roanoke? The answer to this question is that we simply have no idea, but one could speculate that since this was White's third voyage, he may have felt the act of sailing over three thousand miles across the Atlantic Ocean was one he was accustomed to and that the journey ahead merely amounted to little more than a trip to the shops, and this may have been the view of those who remained, few, if any, of whom probably had the stomach for undertaking such an arduous voyage again. Whatever the reason, White certainly could have had no comprehension that that 'trip' was to be interrupted by the Spanish Armada!

After the premature relief of the military colony in 1585, the disappearance of Grenville's fifteen men in 1586, and the dumping of the colony in the wrong place in 1587, the year 1588 brought the untimely arrival of the Spanish Armada, quite literally turning up just as Grenville was waiting only for a fair wind to sail from Bideford with a relief fleet for Roanoke!

Before exploring the events of 1588 further, though, it is worth pausing for a moment to realise what an extraordinary year it must have been for the town of Bideford. Picture the quayside, Grenville's newly built house presiding over it. The quay itself was filled with at least three galleons and several other assorted sea-going ships, all being prepared for the relief of Roanoke, and all no doubt under the watchful eye of Grenville. John White, the first governor of Virginia, was perhaps spending his time pacing up and down the quay worrying over the plight of his daughter and grandchild and wondering when they would sail. Rawley, the now baptised Native American Indian, was perhaps busy preparing to make his own hoped-for return to Roanoke, while remaining a source of wonder for the population of the town. Elsewhere, in a quayside public house, Philip Amadas of the 1584 voyage and Grenville's captive pilot Pedro Diaz, perhaps hoping for his own freedom, were probably debriefing the other captains and masters about the intended voyage. To add to the general hustle and bustle of this time, there should be no doubt that the streets of Bideford would have been home to the comings and goings of many of the West Country's landed gentry. The St Legers, the Queen's commanders of Munster in Ireland, the Arundells, one of the most powerful families of Cornwall, and conceivably even Sir Walter Raleigh may well have walked those streets, all being entertained by the Grenvilles at their new house; and all the while, Grenville, perhaps impatient to set sail yet again for the third time in four years, lording over all.

As Grenville and his fleet for Roanoke waited for that fateful break in the weather, news arrived from the Privy Council sequestering that very fleet to be sent to Plymouth under Grenville's command to fight the Spanish Armada, with the precious supplies for Roanoke being removed and replaced by men of war and ammunition.

Yet, Grenville did not forsake his commitment to the Roanoke colony, for he took the delay in waiting for the fight with the Spanish Armada to commence as an opportunity to return to Bideford from Plymouth in order to meet with John White and organise the slipping away of the *Brave* and the *Roe*, ships that also carried a further fifteen male and female colonists for Roanoke.

Yet again, though, the voyage, as so much of the Roanoke saga, was tragically doomed. Ironically, if Pedro Diaz had not escaped via its misfortune, we may not have known so much more of the incredible story that Raleigh's colonisation attempt really was.

By 1589, aware of his permission to develop a colony in Virginia for 'seven years and no more', Raleigh had his assignment drawn up. Its use of legal language has the same effect as today's legal-speak in making it confusing as to who was given what, but what it does give us is the names of possibly two more 'lost' colonists not mentioned in Hakluyt's 1587 account: John Nichols and Humfrey Dimmocke.

By the time 1590 arrived, and with Raleigh no longer officially involved, there was one last desperate attempt to find the colony. As we can see from White's letter of 1593, the arrangements were ill-conceived, with the captains and backers chosen for the task clearly only interested in using the finding of the colony as a flag of convenience under which to conduct their desired, and evidently piratical, activities.

Nevertheless, there are several fragments of interest in White's account of 1590, most to be gleaned once he finally arrived at Roanoke. First, the mention of 'Haunce the Surgeon' from the 1585 voyage and the trench dug by Amadas in 1587 clearly show that there was a substantial nucleus of individuals willing enough to take on the dangers of crossing the Atlantic on more than one occasion for this quest. Philip Amadas, although not on the 1590 voyage, may have sailed to Roanoke at least three times, for example.

Second, when White arrived at the fort on Roanoke, he noted with some surprise how much more strengthened it was than when he had left. This suggests that the colonists must have stayed for some while in order to complete this work, contrary to some sources who suggest that they left almost immediately once White had sailed over the horizon in 1587. Ironically, this strengthening demonstrates just how unlucky the arrival of the Spanish Armada probably was, as it suggests strongly that the period the colonists remained at Roanoke was at least long enough to overwinter 1587/1588 and therefore perhaps also far enough into 1588 to establish whether any relief was coming.

Lastly, from the 1590 voyage we obtain the greatest epitaph of the whole seven years, that of the sign left by the colonists: 'CROATOAN'. White's instruction to the colonists was to leave the message with a simple cross beneath it if they had to flee under duress. No cross was evident, and therefore they clearly left of their own accord. Given the strengthening of the fort, it is conceivable that they left simply because they got tired of the attacks probably being launched against them by followers of Wanchese. In considering this orderly departure as opposed to one of blind panic, we must remember that no graves and no bodies were found by White, nor were there any signs of the houses or palisade being subjected to burning.

White, seeing the sign, was convinced that his colonists had moved to be with the relative safety of the friendly Croatoan Indians down at Hatteras, and that is certainly where he headed next. However, the fateful and stormy intervention by Mother Nature, coupled with the loss of men already sustained whilst trying to land, and yet more men being injured when the capstan gave way, ensured that ultimately it was too much for the fleet to endure. White's captains set sail for Trinidad to overwinter and make repairs, or so White thought. The cruel reality was that this was just a ruse to persuade White that they would return. They never did.

John White last saw his daughter and grandchild in 1587 as he sailed away from Roanoke, his hopes had been raised and dashed in 1588, and now finally in 1590 he found himself sailing away, looking back at Roanoke yet again. By 1593 he had retired to Ireland a broken man.

There remains a fascinating possibility of two further attempts to find the colony. The first may have resulted from a deposition by Darby Glande, the potential colonist stranded during the 1587 voyage, which sent Vincente Gonzalez, a Spanish sea Captain, looking for the colony in 1588. In the original documents Gonzalez only describes an unnamed bay he visited where natives told him of an English settlement to the north *'which had a river flowing into it'* (perhaps meaning they were on an Island in a bay). Such description of course could refer to Roanoke but Glande could only have known that the intended destination of the Colony was Chesapeake Bay, not that they had been deserted by Simon Ferdinando on Roanoke. It seems likely therefore that Gonzalez focused his search on Chesapeake Bay. Ironically, by making his deposition, Darby Glande may well have unknowingly saved the very colony he hoped to be part of.

The second record comes merely as a footnote in John Brereton's account of Bartholomew Gosnold's exploration of New England in 1602 and is entitled *A briefe Note of the sending another barke this present yeere 1602, by the honorable knight, Sir Walter Ralegh, for the searching out of his Colonie in Virginia*. If it did take place, it probably did so without official approval, for there are no court records to confirm it. The footnote reads:

Samuel Mace of Weymouth, a very sufficient Mariner, an honest sober man, who had beene in Virginia twise befoe, was imployed thither by Sir Walter Ralegh, to finde those people which were left there in the yeere 1587. To those succour he hath sent five severall times at his owne charges. Their owne profit elsewhere; others returning with frivolous allegations. At this last time, to avoid all excuse, he bought a barke, and hired all the company for wages by the moneth: who departing from Weymouth in March last 1602, fell fortie leagues to the Southwestward of Hatarask, in thirtie-foure degrees or thereabout; and having there spent a moneth; when that the extremitie of weather and loose of some principall ground-tackle forced and feared them from searching the port of Hatarask, to which they were sent.

'Fortie leagues' would place Samuel Mace's landing place somewhere around Cape Lookout, as it is known today, at least sixty miles south of Hatteras (Croatoan). In effect they, too, were evidently beaten back by a probable hurricane, causing the loss of the anchor and other mooring equipment.

Officially or unofficially, Raleigh's imprisonment ensured there were to be no further attempts to find the Lost Colony of Roanoke.

The manner of their fishing

Chapter Fifteen

~

The Hunt for the Lost Colony

So just what did become of the 'lost' colonists? Perhaps, after John White disappeared over the horizon, the colonists decided to stay at least long enough for him to return from England. This would mean the colony overwintered on Roanoke expecting a spring visit in 1588. They probably suffered a hard winter, too, with little food and probable continued efforts by Wanchese and his renegades to wipe out their toehold in America, the latter no doubt responsible for the strengthening of the fort at Roanoke.

As 1588 arrived and the summer dragged on without sight of any relief, it is probable that having been worn down by the Indian attacks and with perhaps some of their number having been kidnapped to become slaves for their skills at copper-beating and building, the colony began to fragment. Some may have considered that their best chance of survival was to head north to the Chesapeake Bay, while others may have felt that remaining on Roanoke or nearby Hatteras with the friendly Croatoans offered the best chance of survival. Hatteras also provided the obvious alternative landing place for any English rescue attempt (as White was to prove in 1590).

Whether the split came in the summer of 1588 or early in the spring of 1589 cannot be known. There would surely have been a point where the factions within what remained of the colony settled into distinct groups. At that point, with the weather set fair, perhaps Captain Edward Stafford and some of the planters headed north in the pinnace, up the Currituck Sound bound for the Chesapeake Bay, to become perhaps the makers of those English fields along the James River or the English referred to by the Indians who spoke to Vincente Gonzalez in 1588.

Those who remained at Roanoke probably included most of the families but likely also a great many of the single men from the colony roster. In consideration of this, since the colony shared Roanoke with some of Manteo's people (for this is where Ralph Lane was entertained by Granganimeo's wife) it is not unreasonable to think that several of these single men may have already taken an Indian wife. In effect they became family men themselves.

Nor is it unreasonable to think the English offered the Indian villagers safe haven in their fort during times of attack, thus the interrelationship between the two communities would have been strengthening all the time.

With their military power diminished and the attacks continuing both on the English and the Croatoans, the Indian villagers probably chose to abandon their homes and move south to the relative safety of Hatteras. It seems certain the remainder of the English colony would have asked to go with them, or may simply have been asked if they wished to relocate, too.

When John White called upon Roanoke in 1590, his description of the fort should leave us in no doubt that the colonists had been gone perhaps at least a year. Perhaps for several years following, possibly even a generation or two, the colonists lived peacefully on Hatteras. Ultimately, either famine, natural catastrophe or the Tuscarora War forced the perhaps now much intermarried colonists to disperse to the mainland. If we believe in the so called CORA tree (more of which later), then they moved to the mainland to either join the Coree tribe by Lake Mattamuskeet, or moved into the Beechlands area once part of Coratuck (now Currituck) County. From then on, this group was probably scattered and diluted further by the introduction of a great many more settlers from the expanding north.

As plausible as this seems, the truth is that we have only fragments of accounts from the following 120 years or so that yield any sort of tantalising clue as to what really happened. It is for that reason the Lost Colony remains one of America's greatest mysteries.

All things considered, it seems extraordinary that there were no further searches conducted for the Roanoke colonists, not even when John Smith sailed up the James River and noted English-style fields leading up from the riverbanks. Nor was Smith later provoked to explore them when Powhatan, father to Pocahontas, presented him with a matchlock and several other English artefacts, claiming that these were proof his tribe had wiped out the first English settlers in the area.

Sometime following Powhatan's claims, however, an unsupported story surfaced stating that some of the English were in the very fields seen by Smith at the time of the attack. The story continues that in seeing the impossible odds stacked against them, the colonists simply fled into the river to hide among its reed beds until the danger had passed. More than a hundred years later, people living on some of the islands in the Chesapeake Bay were noted as speaking in an Old English accent.

A few years later, in 1612, William Strachey reported the existence of native Indians discovered living in houses built of stone. He further reported the sighting of several white adult males, some boys and a young girl seen working copper in another Indian settlement. Yet no one appears to have made any effort to seek confirmation of these extraordinary stories.

Nearly a hundred years passed before John Lawson, a land surveyor exploring the Outer Banks region of North Carolina, visited Roanoke in 1701 and recorded this of the island:

(Roanoke) where the Ruins of a Fort are to be seen at this day, as well as some old English Coins which have been lately found; and a Brass-Gun, a Powder-Horn, and one small Quarter deck-Gun, made of Iron Staves, and hoop'd with the same Metal; which Method of making Guns might very probably be made use of in those Days, for the Convenience of Infant-Colonies.

He then travelled sixty miles south to Hatteras and had this to say of that visit:

These (Indians) tell us, that several of their Ancestors were white People, and could talk in a Book, as we do; the

Truth of which is confirm'd by gray Eyes being found frequently amongst these Indians, and no others. They value themselves extremely for their Affinity to the English, and are ready to do them all friendly Offices.

Lawson adds the following hypothesis to his account:

It is probable, that this Settlement miscarry'd for want of timely Supplies from England; or thro' the Treachery of the Natives, for we may reasonably suppose that the English were forced to cohabit with them, for Relief and Conversation; and that in process of Time, they conform'd themselves to the Manners of their Indian Relations.

However, even given the revelations of his observations, Lawson did not publish details of his explorations of the area (the book was entitled *A New Voyage to Carolina – See Reference 8*) until 1709, and even then, it was only originally published in England. Sadly, the events of the 1580s had long since been forgotten, and thus the significance of Lawson's accounts of the area simply went unnoticed.

Within six years of the publication of Lawson's work, the entire native Indian population of the Outer Banks area became embroiled in the bitter Tuscarora Indian War of 1711 - 1714. Thus, any prospect of making further discoveries about those Hatteras Indians largely disappeared. Whatever fragment remained of the Croatoan population following that war, they evaporated into the ether of the emerging European immigrations that were by now spreading rapidly through North Carolina.

It is not until the American Civil War that there are any further records providing evidence of Raleigh's colony, and even these exist only in the form of maps vaguely pointing to pre-existing forts among those built during that war. Ironically, we now know that the erection of at least one of those forts resulted in some destruction of the now invaluable archaeology left behind by both the military colony of Ralph Lane and possibly John White's Lost Colony.

Almost another century passed until the 1930s, when American playwright Paul Green wrote the *The Lost Colony*, a play still regularly performed to packed audiences on Roanoke today. The play's popularity was further fuelled by the creation of the national park around most of the northern end of the island of Roanoke. This, complete with the proclamation that Payne's Civil War fort was actually that of Ralph Lane's, and the discovery of several fragments of period archaeology apparently confirming that the Lost Colony had indeed been found, all added to the illusion.

However, while Roanoke's claims to be the first English settlement in America are indisputable, at the time of writing, the evidence from the archaeology is still wholly inadequate to prove the locations of any of Lane's forts, the colony's village, or indeed the colony's visitations or removal to any other location mentioned in the original transcriptions. Any such claims therefore to having 'found' the colony must remain on very tenuous ground.

What physical evidence the lost colony left behind is limited to only a handful of possibilities:

1. The discovery of Lane's forts either on Roanoke or at Port Ferdinando (Bodie Island).

2. The discovery of the pinnace now thought to have been left with the colony.

3. The discovery of identifiable skeletal remains or personal belongings of the colonists. In this respect personal effects of the female 'lost' colonists would be preferable as they could not be subjected to claims of belonging to the earlier voyages, all exclusively the preserve of men.

4. Confirmation of the clues many believe the colonists deliberately left behind.

Taking each possibility in turn, let us first review the search for Lane's forts. If the earthwork at the National Park Service's centre on Roanoke is not Lane's fort, then where is it? The best assessment of this, given Lane's penchant for building by the water's edge, is that either the significant erosion that has taken place on the northeast tip of Roanoke means it is now underwater, ironically placing the fort's location close to the present-day site of the Lost Colony theatre, or that it is on the more stable northwest corner of Roanoke.

In any event, it is unlikely that Lane's fort remains as anything significant in the form of raised earthworks, thus its formal identification is likely to be a lengthy task. Nevertheless, it is a prize archaeologists are only too well aware of, especially given that it also served as the colonists 'Cittie of Ralegh'. It is therefore not inconceivable that this prize will one day be finally discovered, as indeed it must.

Lane's other fort on the Outer Banks, Port Ferdinando on Bodie Island, has never been sought. Yet, since Bodie Island is uninhabited even today, despite no longer being an island, one would think that this fort is more likely to remain reasonably intact and therefore easier to identify.

What then of the pinnace captained by Edward Stafford? All we can conjecture about it is to suggest that if you were a colonist of 1587 and you knew, as they did, that the intended destination for the English settlement was due north along the very route that Lane had taken two years previously, would you not have attempted to reach that location? Especially given the rose-tinted account that Barlowe, Lane and others had written about it. If those colonists did indeed attempt to make that journey in the pinnace then it is likely that either today's Great Dismal Swamp National Wildlife Refuge holds the clues, for this is where that ship would probably have come to ground and been abandoned if they had taken Lane's route, or else it lies somewhere along the coast or in the Chesapeake Bay, the latter assuming the colonists did indeed make it to their desired destination.

An alternative possibility is that it was used to ferry the colonists around the Pamlico and Albemarle sounds, a combined area that, whilst filled with shallows, is at least thirty-five miles across at its widest point and around a hundred miles in length, thus making the pinnace invaluable. There is one last, perhaps obvious theory though. The ship had made it to Roanoke from England, and therefore perhaps it was reasonable to think she could make the return journey. There is no record of her return or that of her shipwrecked crew being saved. If such a voyage was made, the ship and all those onboard perished in the attempt.

Finding Stafford's pinnace could give us the clearest possible indication of where the colonists headed after deserting Roanoke. Sadly, given the vastness of the area we would need to search, and the likelihood of the pinnace's decay over the centuries, the chance of its discovery remains remote.

We come now to the possibility of the survival of personal effects or skeletons belonging to the colonists. First, we must deal with the subject of skeletal remains. The discovery of such could provide DNA by which to compare today's hoped for descendants, but of much more significance perhaps would be to hope that any such skeletal remains included teeth.

Tooth enamel forms in a child's first few years, so it stores a chemical record of the environment in which the individual grew up. Two chemical elements are found in teeth enamel - oxygen and strontium.

Most of the oxygen in teeth and bone comes from drinking water. In warm climates, drinking water contains a higher ratio of heavy oxygen (O-18) to light oxygen (O-16) than it does in cold climates. So comparing the oxygen isotope ratio in teeth with that of drinking water from different regions can provide information about the climate in which a person was raised. We then come to the strontium. Most rocks carry a small amount of the element which permeates into the water table. The ratio of strontium 87 and strontium 86 isotopes varies according to local geology. Testing the isotope ratio of strontium in a person's teeth can provide information on the geological setting where that individual lived in childhood. By combining the results from both tests, archaeologists can gather data pointing to regions where a person may have been raised. The results for someone raised on the Outer

Banks of North Carolina will be substantially different from those of someone raised in England.

Given that it seems a fair assessment to state that any surviving colonists probably integrated with the native Indians, possibly in as little as a generation or two, it is wholly unrealistic to expect to find a recognisable 'English' grave complete with grave marker. The Indian form of burial, whilst detailed in its preparation, ultimately amounted to the remaining bones being disposed of in a simple pit. The oxygen and strontium tests therefore could prove whether any skeletal remains are English, or Native American.

One of the most extraordinary finds relating to possible skeletal remains concerns the finding of a burial casket, four burial caskets in fact, for this is precisely what was found some decades ago in an area known as Beechlands, just a few miles into the mainland from Roanoke. The story has been recounted numerous times and yet the exact location of the find has been lost, like so much else relating to the colony. Essentially the story goes that while excavating a channel through the area, the operator of an excavator uncovered four, possibly five, wooden caskets, each of which had been made by inverting two canoes and pegging them together. The operator, according to some sources, even stated that the caskets had a Romanised 'cross' on them and the initials INRI inscribed upon them. When he told his supervisor of his find, the supervisor's immediate reaction was to deduce that they had stumbled upon an unmarked cemetery and the caskets were quickly reburied in rather indecent haste. Today, no one knows where that burial place is. Whether they were indeed 'lost' colonists or simply other unidentified early explorers or settlers, we simply do not, and may never, know.

So what of personal possessions? Recent archaeological excavations led by the Croatoan Archaeological Society with Professor Mark Horton and the author, identified many items of English origin, most of which were uncovered in context with native Indian artefacts. These finds included fragments of belt and shoe buckles, firing mechanisms from Matchlocks, possible sword or dagger fragments and a vast range of pottery sherds. Although none of the items can yet be positively identified as 16th century in origin, many of them represent clear evidence of English influence some time before land grants were issued to migrant settlers in the 18th century. Of particular note among the finds though, is the substantial amount of English and European pottery, some of which is identifiable as being slipware from North Devon, a pottery also found widely around Jamestown, but of particular significance to the Lost Colony given the likely origin of many of its settlers. Interestingly, the accuracy of the dating we have for some of the pottery fragments is enough to demonstrate that they pre-date John Lawson's survey of 1701 by several decades.

So, just how did these fragments come to be on Hatteras? If the islanders, perhaps much inter-married by the mid-17th century, traded for them, then there are no records of a blue-eyed, English-speaking Indian wandering into an English township to do so, regardless of the sensation that would have created. We could assume that either traders visited the area but made no mention to others of the 'blue-eyed' Indians they traded with, or, perhaps far more logically, these fragments were from ships wrecked on their way to trade in the English settlements further north.

Among the other finds, the most striking items have to be the range of early (pre-1650) English clay pipes uncovered, the unique use of kaolin in their manufacture marking them out as English. We know the Indians smoked a wild form of tobacco but they had their own, far more robust native pipes. Why then would they want English pipes? Was it a hankering in their old English genes?

No mention of personal artefacts would be complete, however, without raising the spectre of the so-called Kendall ring. This was a famous find of the last decade which has remained largely hidden from public eyes until very recently. The claim is that the gold ring, which contains the alleged image of a Kendall family coat of arms on its face, was dropped by Master Kendall of the military colony. Analysis of the image on the ring, which appears as a stylised lion, does not match either of the coats of arms of the two known Kendall families of the period. Whilst authorities dispute the Kendall connection, the ring's age could be determined by isotope dating of a tiny fragment, but this request of what many Americans see as pivotal and precious evidence in the search for the colonists has yet to be granted and is not likely to be an easy one for them to agree to. Given that the construction of the ring makes it a strong candidate for being of Elizabethan origin, this is a frustrating situation.

Finally, we come to the possible clues deliberately left behind by the colonists themselves, and these number perhaps just two.

The first discovery has become known as the Eleanor Dare Stones. These give a plausible account of the life and times of Virginia Dare's mother, Eleanor, marrying an Indian chieftain following the death of her husband, Ananias, and then having another daughter by that chief, called Agnes. When the first stone was uncovered in 1937, sixty miles west of Roanoke, it caused a sensation. Over the following years forty-seven more came to light, some of which were found over five hundred miles away in modern-day Georgia.

The fundamental issue with the stones, however, is one of authenticity. For example, the language used on the stones is inconsistent with the style and prose of Elizabethan English. Paul Green, the author of the play *The Lost Colony*, also stated that the story related by the stones largely followed that of his play. Curious, then, that the colonists knew what variations Paul Green would put into his play 350 years before it was written!

The stones have been further blighted by the involvement of several known hoaxers being linked to their discovery; this fact alone naturally calls their entire authenticity into question. It is perhaps worth noting about this sorry episode, though, that the first stone found is quite different in many respects from those later brought forward for public scrutiny. Yet the authenticity of it, like the other forty-seven, which all still exist in a private collection today, remains unproven.

The second discovery relates to another tree with an inscription etched into its trunk. We may no longer have the post or tree with 'CRO' or 'CROATOAN' on it but we do have the 'CORA' tree sixty miles south on Hatteras. It is unquestionably an ancient tree into whose trunk the word 'CORA' is carved, now distorted with age. Could this have been carved by a 'lost' colonist? It is in the same English-capital style as would be expected of the Elizabethan period, and it is clearly etched deep enough to be several hundred years old. The 'Cora' referred to could just be a reference to the Coree tribe who's last settlement of an estimate 125 souls was located by Lake Mattamuskeet on the nearby mainland. If the colonists relocated to Hatteras and then subsequently moved to the mainland, was the word 'CORA' carved deliberately into that tree as part of their continuing effort to leave a sign in the hope of being found? As with all finds relating to the Lost Colony though, the name 'CORA' is also credited to a story of the hanging of a female named Cora from this tree, sometime in the eighteenth century!

For all the physical evidence now being uncovered, archaeology can ultimately only tell us where they lived and how they lived and died. It can never tell us if any of their descendants are alive today, and it is this facet, if proven, that will need to be determined if we are to rewrite the history of America.

* * *

So just how do we prove that survival of descendants?

The most logical starting point would be to delve into the archives of England to see if any ancestral connections can be found with those living today. The problem is that when you review the colonists' surnames, one has to ask, just where would you start searching for names like Smith (as in Thomas Smith) and Jones (as in John Jones)? A recent search through the Prerogative Court of Canterbury records for example, revealed around three hundred Wills that could relate to the colonists; yet of the seventy or so studied by the time this book went to print, none have yielded anything that may confirm their connection. It is possible of course that the colonists either simply did not have estates of sufficient value to warrant the Court's involvement, or they literally sold up and took everything they had with them, but the interrogation of these wills does highlight the potential scale of the problem.

Yet the search for these ancestral connections may not be so difficult. Raleigh, Grenville and their followers invested a serious amount of money into the project to colonise America. Such a venture had no option but to rely on the abilities and loyalty of those they sent to do the job 3,500 miles and several weeks' worth of travelling away. In effect their choices had to be restricted to their employees, acquaintances, or perhaps, and just as likely, those of their circle of family and friends. In effect, people they could trust.

It therefore stands to reason that many if not all of the colonists were already known to the principal investors and senior participants of Raleigh's project to settle Virginia. We can confirm this in part by referring to John White's own words, which imply that he felt responsible for those he convinced to go to Roanoke.

However, finding those you can trust to do the job is one thing, convincing them to go is another. Even given that Raleigh offered a generous incentive, a snippet contained in the Domestic State Papers of Elizabeth (27 April 1586) sent from the lieutenants of Cornwall and Devon highlights the problem of persuading people to settle in a foreign land (in this case, Munster in Ireland). That entry states:

We have generally made known through this country, her majesty's offers, and do find none of sufficient ability offer to undertake the same. We suggest it would further the people's willingness if some principal gentlemen of each county, of whose discretion and fidelity the people are persuaded, be sent with them as their captain or Governor, the people then would follow.

In selecting John White and his twelve assistants, the investors chose those they believed could be trusted to govern and administer the colony. John White and his assistants in turn then, may have known or been known to many of the remaining hundred or so colonists who sailed with them to America.

One further compelling argument for this theory comes from looking at the demographics of many of the surnames. If we look closely, we can determine just how they may relate to Raleigh and his circle of investors, thus proving that they may have been signed up from an exclusive group of individuals. What the surname study reveals is some interesting patterns centred on the West Midlands, south-western Scotland, southern Ireland, south and west Somerset, west Dorset, Devon, Cornwall and finally, two at present rather disassociated areas, Portsmouth and Lincolnshire. Taking each area in turn and beginning with the latter two, this is what we find:

There is no obvious connection between Raleigh and

his circle of friends and Portsmouth, but this could be down to one simple fact. The fitting out of the ships here for a voyage to plant a colony in Virginia would have been common knowledge among the townsfolk, as significant numbers of them would have been called upon to supply victuals, etc. Given that Raleigh was well short of colonists even when finally sailing, we should accept that some of the colonists may simply have travelled as a result of speculative enquiries being made of the ships' captains.

The nucleus of colony surnames largely exclusive to the Lincolnshire area may have arisen because of Hakluyt's advice for good builders; the Lincolnshire style of house building was highly regarded at the time.

We move now to areas where there could be grounds for suggesting a link to the colony's investors. The West Midlands colony surname connection may come through the Earl of Shrewsbury, someone who was certainly known to Raleigh and Grenville. George Talbot, then Earl of Shrewsbury, had a flagship called the *Talbot* of some two hundred tons which took part in Drake's West Indian adventure, the same adventure that relieved Ralph Lane's Military colony from Roanoke in 1585.

The connection with the south-western area of Scotland had been puzzling the author for a long time, until a recent discussion with Professor Mark Horton, who has studied early Scottish migratory patterns, revealed that it seems likely that the appearance of Scottish surnames in the colony might be due to religious persecution. In the late 1500s Scotland was still a country in its own right under Mary, Queen of Scots; a staunch Roman Catholic. There can be no doubt therefore that many Protestants were evicted from their lands because of their beliefs. Sir Walter Raleigh knew of their plight and had connections with the west coast area of Scotland. It seems likely that given his need to populate his Irish estates during the 1570's, he may have taken a ready-made colony from the west coast of Scotland and transplanted it to his estates around Cork in southern Ireland. Here we must recognise that Grenville, Raleigh's in-law, also had several estates. The State Papers for Ireland confirm this, for they contain records of Grenville also populating his lands with ninety-nine settlers; settlers that almost certainly came from his West Country estates. It is not unrealistic to consider that as the settlements in southern Ireland (Munster) began to turn sour, both Raleigh and Grenville persuaded some of these colonists to move again, this time to Virginia.

In west and south Somerset, west Dorset, Devon and Cornwall, we find the country seats of some of the most pivotal players and investors in the colony: Grenville, Raleigh, the Earl of Dorset (who later laid claim at the Prerogative Court of Canterbury to being the rightful ward of one John Dare, son of Ananias), the Harris family of Plymouth, the Arundells of Cornwall, the St Legers of Annery (near Bideford) and various others. We must also remember that many of the West Country gentry were related. There are numerous records of Grenville spending time with his cousins in Cornwall for example. Those records also include others who, while they may not have been named investors, would have been in the sphere of influence for recruitment, for example the Bassetts of Umberleigh in Devon who also owned land at Tehidy in

Cornwall, the Vyell's, the Godolphins and so on. Fertile ground indeed for finding potential colonists.

However, even given this evidence, a great many who have studied the origins of the colonists believe they came almost exclusively from London. Pedro Diaz, after all, does state in his deposition that Grenville travelled to London to obtain 210 people for the colony in Virginia. As much as one might consider London the obvious choice however, there are good reasons to cast a note of caution on this hypothesis.

London was fashionable and a Mecca for the landed gentry (witness the names Raleigh quotes as being the investors and 'gentlemen' participants of the venture). Yet in almost every case, these people had estates in the country and simply used London as a giant commercial and communication hub, which is effectively what it was, a central meeting place where business was conducted. Furthermore, such a large population would hardly know of any such venture to Virginia (and sign up for it on a whim) without some form of mass marketing. Do we have any posters advertising the voyage? Any parish records of the dozens of communities in London being asked for volunteers? Is there anything in the London guilds, such as the guild of painters and stainers or the clothmakers' guild, for example, recording the request for volunteers of specific trades as recommended by Hakluyt? In short, with such widespread potential for sources of evidence, it would be surprising if nothing survived to support this theory. Yet there is nothing.

We could consider that some may have been working indirectly for the investors, for example as bookkeepers of a London-based accountancy practice, and thus any canvassing may have been conducted by word of mouth.

However, given that being a favoured courtier at the Elizabethan court was fickle at best, with regular stories of deceit and treachery, it is hardly likely that any prominent individual whose downfall might result in the promotion of another at court, or worse, result in the dismantling of their estates to the benefit of that rival, would have entrusted their personal finances to, say, Roger Bailie & Co. Accountants, for fear of that company being owned or influenced by a more powerful enemy. Nevertheless, if this was the case and such generic institutions were used, it seems hardly likely that these institutions would allow their valuable and trusted employees to go to Roanoke without some return from the colony investors. Yet, like so much else of the London theory, there are no known records of any such correspondence or agreements.

Nor are there any records of sailings from the port of London, something we would expect if this was indeed the port of departure. The only recorded ports of departure for any of the Roanoke voyages are Portsmouth, Plymouth and Bideford. Are we to believe that men, women (two of whom may have been pregnant), and their children simply made their way to Portsmouth from London, complete with their worldly goods? Or is it more likely that many were sat waiting quietly on the quayside further down the coast at Plymouth, having made their way there courtesy of their employers local trade routes?

If we investigate this demographic theory further, we get some intriguing results.

Take colonist Thomas Smith, for example. One of the

earliest records we have is that of the Smith family of Bideford (home of Grenville). In 1696 the Smiths of Bideford set up a shipbuilding yard on the Chester River in the state of Maryland to serve the ships collecting tobacco from their own plantations in Virginia. Could one of their ancestors barely a hundred years previously have been a shipwright? More Bideford, and thus Grenville, connections could be from those other shipbuilders associated with the town, the Chapmans and the Ellises. Is it conceivable that Thomas Ellis, his son Robert, and John Chapman worked on converting Grenville's prize Spanish ship of 1585 into the *Dudley* and later joined Thomas Smith to sign up for the Roanoke colony, perhaps even at Grenville's request? What too of Henry and Richard Berrye, gentlemen with a surname famous among Bideford maritime heroes? The surname is also linked to several estates in the area, not least Eastleigh Manor barely two miles from Bideford and home to the Berrys between circa 1500 and 1800. We must remember that for Roanoke to prosper it was essential that shipbuilding and maritime navigation skills existed among the colonists. This is just one example in one associated area, of course, but it does provide a tantalising clue to how and where we may find the English origins of the 'lost' colonists.

In searching for those colonists we must, however, ensure that the most pivotal name remains a priority in our quest: that of Ananias Dare. For it was he who fathered the first born American, Virginia Dare, a daughter who we should be certain was watched over vigilantly by whatever remained of the colony. There has been widespread speculation that Ananias Dare came from Cambridgeshire or Essex, but could he not be related to the Dares of Lyme Regis on the border of Dorset and Devon, an area central to the influence of Raleigh and the Earl of Dorset? Ananias Dare's Christian name makes for easy discovery among the fragments of early English parish records. There are indeed only three records known to date: a christening from Plymouth; a christening for North Curry in Somerset, and lastly a marriage (apparently to Eleanor White, John White's daughter) in London. But that's it. This is all we have to date. We know nothing of his life, there is no evidence to support popular claims of his involvement with one of the London guilds, and he has no known address. What we do have amounts to but two connections, firstly his connection to John White through the marriage to his daughter, and the remote possibility that the Martin Dare connected to Sir Richard Grenville was a relative.

Given the focus of research on the colonists who remained on Roanoke, it's not surprising that the colony's Principal, John White has largely been overlooked. Apart from his position as father to Eleanor and grandfather to Virginia, he appears to offer no further connection to the hunt for descendants of those colonists. Yet this is not true. You have already read about how he felt responsible for persuading many to go to Virginia and thus he clearly knew some of the colonists. If we can find out who he was therefore, we may yet find more clues as to who the colonists were.

So what of John White? If we allow for his daughter's probable age at marriage we can estimate a date of birth for him of around 1540. He was then, similar in age to

Grenville. With this date of birth in mind, a trawl through the English archives reveals more than twenty prospective candidates who could be our John White. Amongst these there are several with strong claims.

Our first candidate is one such John White whose last will and testament tells us he was a merchant of Bideford who died in 1583, leaving money to his son, also called John White, and his daughters. It was a very timely inheritance if one wished to speculate in a venture to Virginia. Indeed it was also the year Eleanor White married Ananias Dare in London, a record of which we find in the parish registers of St Clement Dane dated 24 June 1583. One final note about this John White is the legacy of a marriage recorded in the Bideford parish register involving one 'Elinor' White on 12 February 1615. It was customary back then to name a new member of the family in remembrance of another son or daughter. Was this Eleanor named after a lost daughter also called Eleanor White née Dare? Frustratingly no record of this particular Eleanor's birth or christening has yet been found.

The second candidate is from St Germans, near Plymouth. The Whites of this parish lived close enough to Sir Richard Grenville during his childhood to have probably been known to him. The family was also wealthy and had London connections. Indeed, a John White, 'citizen and haberdasher of London', created a charity for the poor of St Germans in 1587, a very timely date. If this John White had a daughter called Eleanor then also living in London, it could add credibility to the marriage entry of Ananias Dare to Eleanor White also discussed in the previous paragraph.

Our third candidate may have come from an estate owned by a White family of Somerset. This has prospects as the estate could have been within a few miles of North Curry, a possible location for the birthplace of Ananias Dare. Ananias had to court Eleanor White, John's daughter, somewhere, and the Somerset location provides the potential for how they may have met.

Yet another John White comes from a wholly unrelated location but one which should not be dismissed without further investigation. He could have originated from Cumbria, or more precisely Westmorland. Certainly a White family of some prominence lived in the area at the time and were known to have had connections with the John Peel of folk-song fame. Yet perhaps most telling of all is that the Westmorland area was home to the Earls of Cumberland. Through their prominent attendance at the Elizabethan court, this family would unquestionably have come into contact with Raleigh and Grenville and their plans for Virginia.

Without wishing to labour a point, we could go on to include John White, Lord of the Manor of Southwicke (conveniently near Portsmouth) who is known to have had a daughter called Bridget. A 'Bridget' is named as an executor of a John White who died in Ireland (where our John White was known to be in 1593) in circa 1607. We could also add John White who was Lord Mayor of London and not only had two sons also called John White, but was a member of the Company of Merchant Venturers, an organisation intrinsically involved with exploration and settlement of new lands for financial gain.

Given that John White was the first Governor of

Virginia, governor of the first English colony in America, and grandfather to the first born American, the prize for the English town that proves to be his birthplace should not be underestimated.

***

There will come a time when we may finally have found a likely English candidate with a respectable ancestral claim to being a descendant of a colonist who sailed from England. Once we have that candidate, the next step will be to sample their DNA for matching against an American whose own researched ancestry lays claim to their being a descendent of a lost colonist.

Today, genealogists use DNA and the technology associated with it to examine and provide conclusive and irrefutable evidence in unravelling many of history's great questions. In recent times, for example, it has been used to confirm the identity of the father of the Egyptian pharaoh Tutankhamen. At a lower level, a DNA test resulted in the discovery of two people living over three thousand miles apart, whose common ancestor had sailed from Bideford to start a new life on Prince Edward Island over three hundred years ago. This technology therefore can provide convincing evidence to support any claim of ancestry from the 'lost' colonists by those living today. However, in order to do that, we need to first find the families in England who are related to the colonists, and specifically, those who descend from a common male ancestor sharing the same surname and thus sharing the 'Y' chromosome. The 'Y' chromosome being the portion of the DNA gathered (using a cheek swab) for this type of genealogical DNA testing. The Lost Colony Research Group is responsible for the project and is actively encouraging English families to take part.

(Further information on the project can be found at: www.familytreedna.com/public/LostColonyYDNA/)

They point out that a match with an American family with the same surname, who have an oral history of the Lost Colony, would be compelling evidence to dig further and deeper into English records in the hunt for a colonist family connection. Ultimately, if we can prove a genealogical connection to the colonists in England, and a DNA match to a Lost Colony claimant in the US, then the argument for the colonists' survival may become irrefutable.

Significant steps in DNA testing have already been made in America. The best candidates discovered so far appear to be the descendants of the Croatoan, later known as the Hatteras, Indians who lived on Hatteras Island, and the Lumbee Indians, both of whom hold a consistent oral history of descent from the Lost Colony. Both of these groups are being documented by Roberta Estes in the Lost Colony and Hatteras Families DNA projects. The Hatteras Indians are known to have migrated to the mainland of Hyde, later Dare County, in North Carolina and are known to have been incorporated into the Coree or Mattamuskeet Indians. The Lumbee, found in Robinson County, have documented connections to the Black River area of North Carolina which could be the migration path from the Hatteras coastal area to Robinson County. Testing of descendants of these tribes is important to the ongoing research into the fate of the Lost Colony, as it seems certain that if there are descendants of the lost colonists alive today, they would most likely be found among the descendants of these Indian tribes.

As can be seen from earlier in this chapter, the complexity of England's fragmented web of ancestral records is going to make the process of finding candidate English families with a pedigree of sufficient interest to make the DNA tests worthwhile a long process. Once found, we then have to find their match in America, a match which of course may not yet have found its way into the current database!

Our quest to prove or disprove the survival of the lost colonists could be resolved in a few months, a few years or perhaps even longer. As Professor Mark Horton famously reminded one newspaper who questioned the search for the Lost Colony, it took Howard Carter twenty years to find Tutankhamen. We have only just begun.

* * *

As we plan our next archaeological digs in search of the Lost Colony, and the hunt for suitable DNA candidates continues, I find myself casting my mind back to the first time I walked along the shores of Hatteras (Croatoan) Island, as those colonists must have all those years ago, and asking myself...

What if just one colonist did survive from those left on Roanoke in 1587? What if they survived and prospered long enough to raise a family, who in turn raised their own families, families whose descendants survive to walk the shores of America today just as they did more than four hundred years ago?

We would then know that the Lost Colony did not perish in vain. We would know that they did achieve their objective of founding a new colony. A colony that was founded thirty-three years before the Mayflower set sail and twenty years before Jamestown was built; and one that will rewrite the history of America.

As for Sir Richard Grenville, let us hope, that at last, he too receives the recognition he deserves; for without him, I doubt the story of the 'Lost' Colony of Roanoke would ever have been written.

References

1. Quinn, David B. (1955) *The Roanoke Voyages, 1584-1590*. Hakluyt Society, 2nd series no. 104. London: Hakluyt Society

2. Drinkwater, Bethune C. R. (1847) *The Observations of Sir Richard Hawkins, Knt., in his voyage into the South Sea in the Year 1593*. Reprinted from the edition of 1622 Hakluyt Society, 1st Series no. 1. London: Hakluyt Society

3. Rowse, A. L. (1937) *Grenville of the "Revenge"*. The Bedford Historical Series. 1940. London: Jonathan Cape

4. Dawson, Scott (2009) *Croatoan, Birthplace of America*. Infinity Publishing

5. Hakluyt, Richard (1584) *A Discourse Concerning Western Planting*. Cambridge, Massachusetts: John Wilson Press. 1877. The text was first written in 1584 but was lost for over 300 years until it was first published in 1877.

6. Frankenburg, Dirk (1995) *The Nature of the Outer Banks: Environmental Processes, Field Sites, and Development Issues, Corolla to Ocracoke*. The University of North Carolina Press

7. Stick, David (1990) *The Outer Banks of North Carolina 1584-1958)* The University of North Carolina Press

8. Lawson, John (1701) *A New Voyage to Carolina*. Imprintted London: 1709